A WOMEN IN HORROR POETRY COLLECTION, VOLUME II

Under her Eye

EDITED BY LINDY RYAN & LEE MURRAY

ISBN Print: 978-1-64548-137-9
ISBN Ebook: 978-1-64548-138-6

Cover Design and Interior Formatting by Qamber Designs and Media
Cover art © by Lynne Hansen
www.LynneHansenArt.com

Published by Black Spot Books,
An imprint of Vesuvian Media Group

Over one in four women experience intimate partner violence before the age of 50.

Sardinha, Lynnmarie, Mathieu Maheu-Giroux, Heidi Stöckl, Sarah Rachel Meyer, and Claudia García-Moreno. "Global, Regional, and National Prevalence Estimates of Physical or Sexual, or Both, Intimate Partner Violence against Women in 2018." The Lancet 399, no. 10327 (February 16, 2022): 803–13. https://doi.org/10.1016/s0140-6736(21)02664-7.

Table of Contents

FOREWORD *by Sara Tantlinger*

There is so much power to be found in horror poetry. *Under Her Eye* features poems that feel like confessions written in the dark or scattered pieces of a half-burned memoir. The dynamic range of poems showcase how much talent exists in horror poetry. It's also an incredibly thoughtful anthology with work from cis women, trans women, and non-binary femmes around the world. These amazing writers have come together to share in a truly special project.

The anthology captures how our fears twist imagination, and how past experiences can paint such gray hazes over the present and future. Yet, hope remains. Sometimes hope comes stained in blood or soft with bruises, but hope on its own is a formidable emotion that can blaze through the bleakest of moments. Within these sinewy verses, readers will find truth that is hard to look away from, but that's why horror is important. It is the genre that can most clearly hold up a mirror to society and reflect the darkest parts back at us. In turn, as writers, we get to choose how we want to tell those stories. Using poetry to focus on domestic horror is something every poet in the anthology accomplishes admirably. No one shies away from using each line and each word to create a lasting impact.

A lot of us know these stories. We know the person who gets told to smile more. We know the woman who is in an abusive situation and her friends say, "why don't you just leave?"—like it's that simple and free of fear. We know someone who was ostracized from their family for daring to be different. We know these stories because so many of us have lived them, yet talking about such situations always comes with danger, with feeling like an itch has crawled beneath our skin and we can never scratch it out. The poets in *Under Her Eye* have unapologetically captured the strong emotions and images for these circumstances and more. I applaud every writer involved in this anthology for so beautifully taking those painful ghosts and smattering them onto the page. There is liberation in these pages, between verses and visceral words. And again, there is hope for something greater, which I think is also highlighted in the partnership of the anthology to donate proceeds in the name of globally ending violence against women.

I'd like to congratulate the editors on their selections. Lindy Ryan and Lee Murray have put together a powerful anthology. I want to note how amazing Lindy and Lee are, too. It's been an honor getting to know these two women in horror over the past few years. They both have approached the horror community with kindness, talent, and a fierce dedication toward uplifting the voices of others. We can all learn from their heartening actions.

There is so much that awaits in *Under Her Eye*. Conversations around generational trauma and on body and home, are common themes that will stand out for many readers. I appreciated the range of feral horror, of women who are ready to tackle the world with teeth and claws, all the way to dealing with pain in a softer way. After all, there is never one way to navigate through this life, and the poets here have beautifully shown us that variety. From award-winning writers to those who may be getting their first poem published, it is an inspiration to read all of the work within and get to know these voices.

Horror, as those of us who write it know, is oddly cathartic. As you read through these poignant poems, I hope you find a little healing along the way. I know I did.

—Sara Tantlinger, Bram Stoker Awards®-winning poet

INTRODUCTION *by Regina Yau*

The Pixel Project is a global virtual volunteer-run 501c3 anti-violence against women non-profit whose mission is to raise awareness, funds, and volunteer power for the cause to end violence against women (VAW) through activism and advocacy at the intersection of social media, new technologies, and popular culture/the Arts. In line with our mission, we launched the *Read For Pixels* campaign a decade ago in recognition of the fact that stories play a vital role in the ongoing global battle to end VAW. Together with over 250 award-winning and bestselling authors from genres as diverse as fantasy, science fiction, horror, romance, mystery, and historical fiction, we deployed the power of fictional stories to raise awareness about VAW among book lovers and to reach people who would otherwise remain ignorant of or hostile to the issue.

When Black Spot Books proposed putting together a poetry collection in benefit of The Pixel Project's anti-VAW work, it was a natural next step for us to expand the scope of *Read For Pixels* to include poetry. Over the past year, co-editors Lindy Ryan and Lee Murray rallied 112 female and non-binary poets from across the world to contribute poems to the collection that would become *Under Her Eye*.

These 112 poets tackle the issue of VAW head-on through snapshot-sized stories in the shape of raw and brutally honest poems where word, verse, metre, and rhyme are deftly interwoven to expose the toxic triumvirate of sexism, misogyny, and VAW. *Under Her Eye* hits the ground running from the first line of Stephanie M. Wytovich's opening poem *Know To Be True* invoking "bleached bruises" and never lets up. This second annual women-in-horror poetry showcase takes the reader on a harrowing journey through the full spectrum of violence inflicted by the patriarchy on women's lives the world over, and the devastating ripple effects of that violence on families, communities, and countries.

Whether you read *Under Her Eye* from cover to cover or choose to dip into it at random points, we hope that the poems within will light a spark of courage in you and inspire you to start breaking the silence surrounding the violence. VAW is a difficult subject to broach with family and friends, so use this collection as your very own conversation starter: ask your local librarian to order it, include it in the reading list for your class if you are an English teacher, suggest that your book club reads it next. Maybe gift a copy to a female friend whom you suspect is a domestic violence victim or a rape survivor, so they know they are not alone.

Even if you get only one person to start taking VAW seriously or help a survivor access the support they need, you will have taken your first step toward changing the world.

It's time to stop violence against women. Together.

–Regina Yau, Founder and President
of The Pixel Project, November 2023

NOTES FROM THE EDITORS

Lindy Ryan

This poetry series began with a singular mission: to showcase works of dark verse from women in horror that speak to issues most pertinent to women and nonbinary femmes. Our first showcase, *Under Her Skin*, centered on body horror and the complicated relationship women have with their bodies. This next installment takes the conversation deeper, to domestic horror and the terror women often experience in their own homes.

The poems included in this showcase are raw, resonant, and, in so many cases, all-too relatable. They are poignant and piercing, visceral and vulnerable. Speaking out loud about domestic horror—of the fear women experience in their homes, in their families, with their partners—is a difficult conversation to have, yes. But it is a critical one, and one worth being uncomfortable with. Every day, women all over the world, in all walks of life, are subjected to the *worst* horrors in the places they should feel the *most* safe. They are abused, beaten, murdered, and often, they are forgotten, ignored, and overlooked.

No more.

It has been an absolute honor to work with the 112 poets who shared their words and bared their souls in this showcase, and it has been a pleasure to work alongside the brilliant Lee Murray as co-editor and our wonderful partners at The Pixel Project, who work so very hard to end violence against women worldwide. Every single woman involved in this showcase is a force of creativity, wisdom, and insight, and I am as proud of this showcase as I am of the community built in the process of bringing this collection to you, dear reader.

We invite you to join us, to raise your voices with us, to stand up, speak up, and show up to help end violence against women worldwide. Whether these poems find you as a survivor of domestic horror, or someone struggling to fight their way out of the dark, we hope that you find strength in these poems, courage to fight back, and a safe harbor in a sisterhood of women-in-arms.

—Lindy Ryan, November 2023

Lee Murray

A friend—let's call her Stacey—messaged me recently. She was confused, she said. Conflicted. Her new partner had yelled abuse at her, and the incident had destabilised her. In public, he was loving and respectful; it was only when the doors were closed that the ugliness appeared. The insidious thing was he claimed it was her fault, tried to turn it around on her. What should she do?

red flags / unseen through rose-coloured glasses

Stacey's dilemma is just one example of the real-life horror faced by women and girls all over the world, and in their homes, the very place they should feel safest, with the abuse coming from people they love and who claim to love them.

seven years old / missing her eyelid / baby doll

The United Nations, in its Global Study on Homicide (2018), attests that "home is the most likely place for a woman to be killed" with more than 137 women estimated to be killed by a partner or family member daily.

her neighbours / never miss a trick / except when it matters

Faced with numbers as haunting as these, how can a collection of horror poetry like *Under Her Eye* possibly help? Stephanie Wytovich, Bram Stoker Awards® winner and one of our featured poets, explains:

"When I began combining horror and poetry, it felt like a homecoming, a safe haven. I was no longer worried about saying something too dark or too grotesque, and it embraced me when

I felt broken or weak and didn't have the ability or desire to rise up and wear the badge of final girl. Essentially, the line I'd felt I'd been walking my entire life slowly began to disappear as I refused to walk on eggshells or speak in hushed whispers. I now felt free to run, to scream, but most importantly, to fight. My poems became centered around themes of violence and death, and while they were, and continue to be, graphic and macabre, they speak to survival and female empowerment, to all those private rituals I do to survive, no matter how big or small."
(Wytovich, Conjuring Strength Through Poetry, *Lit Reactor,* 2020)

When crafted with authenticity and compassion, poetry can inspire these same feelings Wytovich describes in the reader, ultimately offering empowerment and hope to those who find themselves represented in the lines.

Or in the space between the lines.

a woman's slip / uncovered / beneath the floorboards

When author-editor Lindy Ryan mentioned co-editing a book of poetry by women in horror, a follow-up to her acclaimed *Under Her Skin* (with Toni Miller), and focusing on the theme of domestic horror, I jumped at the chance. And as I'd recently written the prose-poem, "The Moon Goddess's Granddaughter" for Regina Yau for the Pixel Project's *Giving the Devil His Due* (edited by Rebecca Brewer), the opportunity to connect these powerhouse women, to combine horror poetry with 'a safe haven' (to borrow Wytovich's words), seemed too important to miss.

of all the men she'd dated / he made the cut

I was humbled by the overwhelming response to our submission call, many more than we could select for this volume. Those we chose to include are brutal and beautiful, suffused with both vulnerability and verve. And while they vary in length, style, structure, approach, and perspective, every poem tells a story as old as time, one that is heart-breaking, shocking, and startlingly real. It was a privilege to have been entrusted with their care.

the first time he hits her / he's sorry / so is she

I hope you enjoy reading *Under Her Eye*, a book of hard edges, blunt objects, and dark places. And I hope, like me, these poems inspire you to *do* better, to *be* better, in the face of domestic violence, that our readers too, are galvanised, "to run, to scream, but most importantly, to fight."

my hands are tied, she said / together, we unpick the knots

–Lee Murray, November 2023

KNOW TO BE TRUE

by Stephanie M. Wytovich (Featured Poet)

These bleached bruises hold the arguments
of a hundred fists, a year's worth of where-were-yous,
countless hours of silent treatments and missed calls,
the front door still locked like your jaw
when you screamed, your name a police report,
an underdeveloped photograph hanging in a room
of red.

Do you think the walls still remember the blood loss?
The way bottles broke, their glass bodies like fireworks,
explosive, enraged. We called it a disagreement,
a misunderstanding. Our neighbors referred to it
as the night of a thousand cuts, your skin a haunted house,
your face a mask of concealer, the wrong shade
of blush on death.

For years, I crawled in a dress made of razors, wore
a perfume made from the sweat of running away,
each mile a missed gunshot, every motel room
a collection of sleepless nights, the burn
of the shower an unwrapping of flesh, red like
my lipstick smearing across the palm
of your hand.

Do you think the windchimes still hold
the sound of my body against the wall?
The way my teeth hit the floor, ice cubes
in a glass of wine? We called it a lover's spat,
an argument. My chest home to an endless
wound, a caged bird, the chalk outline
growing in our bedroom what the floorboards
know to be true.

THE WRITING ASSIGNMENT

by Marge Simon (Featured Poet)

She sits in her prof's office,
holding her manuscript,
At the top, the letter "C".
It is all there, life events,
about four thousand words.
She flips through it again,
holding back tears.

How when she turned ten,
her mother came home from the hospital,
waltzed into the front room
and plunked her newborn on the sofa.
"He's all yours," she said.
And off she went to the Bingo.

How when she was fifteen,
her father came home drunk
as he usually did, and of course
did the dirty to her as he'd done
so many nights, for so many years.
She slapped him.
He beat her up.

How when she was eighteen,
he was about to do the same
to her little brother.
But this time, she had a knife.

"You've set up a great motive,
the idea for a good murder story,"
says her professor. "You need action,
more dialog for this to work.
Read some Ruth Rendell,
see how she sets things up."

She just sits there, not knowing
what to say, so the professor continues,
"What you need to do now is
make it more realistic, something
the reader will find believable."

Father was sitting in the kitchen
when she left for class.
She still has the knife.

SHE CHI GROWS
by Geneve Flynn

She Chi grows in her garden
she turns the soil and plants her seeds
plans the plots and feeds her worms
among mandarin and cumquat boughs
she grows and grows and grows
she's smaller now, than she used to be
frailer, older, grey and bent
but
each green leaf, each fiery chili
each winding vine of bean
they grow and grow and so does she
she straightens with a sigh and smiles
everything in the yard is hers and
she's pulled out all the weeds
that is
until
the knock
the visit
the drop-ins
the useless gifts
the pointed reminders
the texts and notes
I'm still here.
I care.
Know this.
I'm thinking of you.
You are never far from my mind.
And I am never far from you.
Why don't you answer.

Let me in.
Knock.
Knock.
Knock.
so she puts a lock on the gate
something big and solid and brass
and for a very bad moment
her garden shrinks
and so does she
but not for long
she plots and plans and turns the soil
and waits for a chance to feed the worms

"ATTN: PRIME REAL ESTATE OPPORTUNITY!"
by Emily Ruth Verona

Superb starter home for a budding family[1]
that just needs a little love and a few finishes.

Beautiful covered porch with view of the lake;
patio[2] around back perfect for entertaining.

Well-lit front hall leads into cozy living room
with a big bay window and original fireplace[3].

One half bath[4] downstairs with a fresh coat
of paint and a newly installed pedestal sink.

Spacious kitchen includes gas range and revamped
cabinetry, tiles have been removed but not replaced[5].

Three bedrooms and one full bath upstairs,
space enough for a nursery[6] or small home office.

Roof is new and septic is in excellent condition,
central heating and cooling inspected recently[7].

Tours by appointment only. Contact listing
agent for details on property disclosures[8].

---

1. What used to be our family
2. Where the fight started that night
3. There was nowhere to hide, so I crawled inside
4. Mom locked the door, but Dad kicked it in
5. Broken ceramic with blood in the grout
6. My sister cried and cried and cried in her crib
7. After the police tape finally went away
8. They are required to tell you what he did here: it's the law

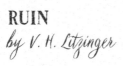

RUIN
by V. H. Litzinger

Hell is a beautiful face—
Its clawed hands bring upon ruin.

I am but human, enticed and seduced by the devil himself,
Honey-filled words sing my praises,
But underneath thorns do grow.

My flesh it is in ruins,
My voice but a whisper,
My eyes are stone,
I—am ravaged

Hell—
Is in my home

RUBIES
by Crystal Sidell

A hurricane of cicadas rattles the windows.
Your parting words rattle my bones:
Don't unbolt the door—no matter what *knocks.*
Hook in hand, I unravel what I've needled.

     Heavy thumps assault the shingle roof.
     My heart thump-thumps against my ribcage.

See this hook? It's no ordinary piece.
It's fashioned onesies, hankies, invisible cloaks.
Crafted by Old World hands.
Handed down from Mother to Daughter.

Azure lightning cracks the wind-whipped sky.
Banging on the kitchen door; stomping cracks the floor.
I'm hungry. Let me in. I need you. Let me in.
It isn't human; I won't be fooled.

     The hour's grown cold; you're probably dead.
     One by one, the lights in the house flicker out.

Trapped in a thunderstorm of darkness—
Agitated cicadas crawling inside every crevice—
Whatever monsters lurk beyond these walls—
I won't be trapped by idleness, by helplessness.

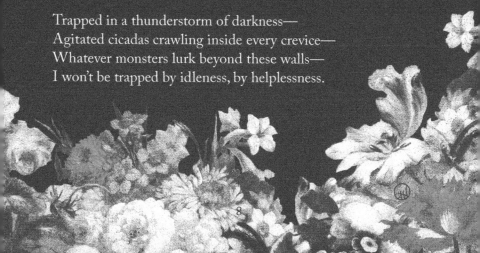

I sit in the dark, working with my hook.
Busy fingers raveling yarn dark as unspilled blood.
Old World fingers raveling things soft yet sharp.
The unlikeliest weapon you'd ever imagine.

    I will tailor my own fate, lassoing energy from this night.
    My heart thump-thumping within my ribcage.

Violent shaking uproots the long-loved oak outside:
Her unsettled roots fling branches through the glass.
I cover my fists with rubies as the inhuman ones crash through.
And if I die? Well… if I die, you'll know I went down fighting.

THE HOUSE SHE WORE
by Caitlin Marceau

No one spoke about the house
my mom wore as a ring,
that was too tight
and cut off her circulation,
from the friends who loved her,
from the family that taught her
to want a husband from the time she was small,
even though she'd always been happier alone.

No one spoke about the house
my mom wore as a dress,
that clung to her body
and highlighted her wide hips,
her sagging stomach,
her drooping breasts,
that changed without her permission
every time her belly swelled and gave him a son.

No one spoke about the house
my mom wore as a pack,
that bent her spine
and got heavier each year,
her shoulders curving,
her body breaking
under a weight that no one helped carry
until she had a daughter, who wore a house of her own.

No one spoke about the house
my mom wore as a shroud,
that covered her body
when she was still alive,
her heart struggling,
her memory failing
in a home she didn't know but had been forced into
by the same people she had been told to love unconditionally.

GROW
by M. Brett Gaffney

Trees don't always look like the green clouds
we drew on construction paper. Not so soft.

And nowhere near as forgiving.

More like veins. More like arms.
Like in *Poltergeist* when the tree attacks
a kid through his bedroom window.

Gnarled branch turned monster claw,
the trunk an open throat.

Spoiler alert: the boy makes it,
but he's never the same.

(Don't even get me started on *The Evil Dead*.)

I know not all trees are terrible,
but some of them can't be trusted.

They talk to each other under our feet.
They unearth the foundation of our house,
the bodies beneath it.

I'm sick of second-guessing gardens.

I want to know a trail of woods
with oaks that leaf understanding—

that know storms and secrets
and the kind of growth
it takes to weather them.

THE VERY WORST KIND OF GHOST
by Tiffany Michelle Brown

I'm hundreds of miles removed
From the apartment in Tucson where it happened,
And yet,

    His jackal-smile is reflected in the dark glass of the microwave,
        Then the hollow plane of the TV before it snaps on,
            Then the chrome handle in my shower.

I've reproduced new cells since then,
Grown new skin,
Toughened my spine and thighs and nerve,
And yet,

    There are stolen moments
        When his guitar-calloused fingertips continue to
            Painfully gouge divots into the soft flesh of my hips.

I've moved eight times,
Packed up chosen memories in cardboard
And bubble wrap,
Greeted new beginnings with open arms,
And yet,

    He's always there.

Because home is not where you sleep,
    Or fold fitted sheets
        Or cook *coq au vin* for special occasions.

It's true what they say,
    Home is where the heart is.

And in that sleepy, desert college town,
    In an apartment he said belonged to a friend,
        With *Event Horizon* playing in the background,

He cracked both my body and heart (home) wide open,
    Forced himself inside,
        Left muddy footprints on the welcome mat.

He continues to overstay his (un)welcome
Because there's a part of him that never leaves.

He is a stain on the dining room wall that can never be erased
    Or painted over
        Or destroyed.

I wonder how many other homes he's broken into,
How many hearts he haunts,

How many times he's found himself
    Embedded in the foundation,
        Lurking under the bed,
            Hiding behind the open refrigerator door,

Never once acknowledging that

He is
The very worst
Kind
Of ghost.

THREATENED ANIMALS
by Elizabeth Anne Schwartz

The personality quiz
asks me to consider
which threatened animal
I most resemble.

And I laugh
at the images
that come to mind,
bizarre and macabre.

The Emperor penguin
in the front seat of your car
while you swerve into oncoming traffic.

The desert cottontail,
alert, all eyes and ears,
making burrows from the holes
your fist carves in the wall.

The pangolin, curled into a ball
in prayer
while the veins pulse in your neck.

Perhaps I was the Tasmanian tiger:
clinging to existence,
jaw stretched wide
as it yowled at the sky.

Perhaps I am the gray wolf:
since I left you,
no longer hunted,
thriving, vivacious
in the mountains
beneath the new moon.

DIRTY SHEETS
by Cassondra Windwalker

shadows eke across the sheets
oozing from under his nails
where my torn skin clumps

regret, black as night,
black as old blood,
stains the pillow where his cheek rests
and he sweats out his grief
almost like a man with a conscience

but when he wakes, he'll remember
how I begged for my bruises,
how he hates the man I make him
with my wild rebellious ways,
and how patiently
he'll school me to repent

I rock the baby and watch him sleep

when he wakes—but he won't,
not this time
sweet cyanide powder on the sheets:
his drunken cells sopping it up
like Jameson, like Tullamore Dew

16

I'll drive to momma's with my one good arm,
give him a couple days to dry out—
the cops in this town feel guilty enough
to not look too hard at alcohol poisonings
what with all the times
they looked away from black eyes:

a little Tide in the wash
and a few hours on the clothesline,
my sheets and my spirit
will show nary a spot.

DATE NIGHT
by Jessica Gleason

The capers popped
in my mouth, tiny
briny little bursts
of flavors.

They pair perfectly
with a timeless
olive-oiled pasta
and a glass of
Sémillon.

Chewing delightfully,
I offer you a taste,
just one delicious morsel
to whet your appetite.

Laughing at my forgetfulness,
I shovel the warm forkful
into my own mouth,
savoring its rich earthy
flavor.

Next time, perhaps,
if you've behaved yourself
we could remove
the tape long enough
for a bite.

THE PEEL
by Dawn McCaig

His wife is not home
Is not due home for an hour
But the glass of water he finds on the table
Her glass, her lipstick on the rim
Is chilled to the touch.
No ice.
Why was she here?
When?
With who?
He sprints to the bedroom
Rips the hand-stitched duvet off their California King
Assesses the sheets.
Twelve hundred thread count
Smooth as butter on hot toast.
Pristine.
The living room is next
The bespoke leather couch
The side chairs (Queen Anne)
Throw pillows
The rug.
Everything in its place.
He would see if it wasn't
But she knows that.
This proves nothing.
He scans the kitchen sink for an extra glass
Opens the dishwasher

Dumps the garbage on the floor.
Orange peels spew out like vomit.
She doesn't like oranges.
So now he knows, someone was here
Consuming the pith
The meat
The flesh

She doesn't like oranges? Maybe she does

The thought is half-formed
A nascent, whining doubt
Weak, like he is, for letting her do this
To him.
He smothers it dead.
Then he waits
For the sound of her footsteps
Flexes his fingers
And wonders
Why does she make me do this?

WAKING UP, I REALIZE
IT IS TIME TO GET OUT
by Syd Shaw

In the dream I am a cow
led to slaughter—he is giving me up.
He is tying me up. We are tired
of each other. I am banished
to the garden, which is
a dollhouse
a slaughterhouse
and also my grandmother's.

He chains me in the yard.
The cars go by, drivers staring,
headlights burning my retinas.
I stomp. I weep. I moo with fury.
I wake up shaking.

With one eye open,
he watches me sweat.
I mumble *yes, yes, I am fine*
so sorry to disturb your sleep.

THESE TINY WOMEN
by Frances Lu-Pai Ippolito

These tiny women
grow taller,
stretching, reaching
each one
each time
you stomp them down.

These tiny women
grow louder,
refusing, spitting out
the icebergs clogging their throats.
Exhaling frozen breaths
to scream their steaming release.

These tiny women
grow sharper
cultivating
a garden of knives
24 blades blooming as ribs in their chests
watered by blood, glutted by pain.

These tiny women
grow freer
protecting, bandaging
one another and another and another
until all of us are safe.

KEPT
by Angela Sylvaine

Chrysalis, transparent as glass
The butterfly emerges
    wings stretching to taste air
A prism of colors so lovely
her beauty snatches the breath from
The Keeper

The world is a danger
    Air thick and polluted
        Sun that burns the delicate
           Hungry predators with sharp beaks
      She must be protected, kept warm and safe and perfect
By her Keeper

She is fed sugar water
    from a glistening bowl
while craving nectar
    from a colorful bloom
Hunger consumes her, she is starved
By her Keeper

The sky calls, tells her
    she is meant to soar and surf the wind
Wings stretch and she flies
    but is stopped by his tether
A snap of her foot, broken
Pain comes but at least she is free
    until she smacks glass erected
By her Keeper

He says she must stay, to be safe
but her hobbled foot will take no tether
She is caged and the window is covered
    There is no more sky
        Wings shrivel and curl
She can only flutter now and sit on the perch provided
By her Keeper

Darkness saps her colors
    muting her beauty to black and gray
Her eyes, going blind, still seek the sun
    a sliver of light beckons
Clumsy and desperate
    she squeezes through the bars
and is snatched from the air
By her Keeper

Her flight is a danger
a temptation she cannot be allowed
He tears off her loveliness
    for her own good
and pins her tattered wings to a board
    a memorial to her beauty
She squirms and cries from the floor of her cage
but she is finally safe
Thanks to her Keeper

LAUNDRY
by Antonia Rachel Ward

i was human once—
a girl, bright-eyed and full of dreams
then I met your father,
a man who thought deep thoughts
while he thought them,
i did his laundry

he wrote,
i sorted socks
hc invented worlds,
i wiped tables
he designed philosophies,
i fed the babies

day after day,
job after job,
he became more solid,
more complex,
and I—

faded

i had to search for myself again,
uncovering one piece at a time
in corners
amongst the dust

now it's just the two of us,
my not-so-little boy
you've grown up a fine man,
a man with dreams,
a man who thinks deep thoughts

and while you think them,
i do your laundry

ONLY THE DEVIL KNOWS
by Kerri-Leigh Grady

when morning alarms woke us for school
mommy stared hard at me and shook her head

what were you up to last night?

sleeping
with kitty who purred me to dreamtime
and super-soft Lamby I stole from my sister
dreaming
of devils who lurk in the hallway
but won't come too near unless I'm asleep

mommy leaned closer and murmured surprise
at dusty smudges speckling my neck

why does it look like hickies?

laughter
chased her back down the hallway
I mounted the stool to see what she meant
bruises
like fingerprints marred my pale skin
like Thing danced in clogs across my poor throat

what could have left such a strange calling card
was it dollies or sisters or devils in dreams

and what was I up to last night?

NO GIRLFRIEND OF MINE
by Blaise Langlois

a knight in shining armour
willing and ready to protect
what is his
tells me
no girlfriend of mine will

no girlfriend of mine will
smile at men on the subway
(I'm only being polite)
walk to class with a guy
(we've known each other since we were three)
wear a thong in tight pants
(but it's just underwear)

he tells me
that I am his
tells me
that he will always be around
and I
believe what he tells me
now

SMILE
by Alexis Clare

they cut your face up
they punch you in the gut
they pierce you
when you tell them to stop
they tell you to keep it
they tell you to give it up
they hit you until your eyes water
and they tell you not to cry
they scream at you
every day
wanting every piece of you
they break you off at the ankles
and they then tell you
to smile

REVERSE FIGHT
by Wendy Booy deGraaff

The drywall releases the punch
of words, unfolds into flat

matte paint with only the tiniest
nick of missing blue. The pillow

releases the wet of sobs screamed
into it. The words swallow back down

to the nether regions. The synapses
disconnect. You go back outside, back

down the sidewalk, back to wherever
you were when you became angry,

back through time and memories, back
to wet and wiggly baby, pulling into

the birth canal and up into your mother's
uterus where the gods bestow different

genes into those curling strands of DNA.

THE COLOR OF BRUISES
by Mercedes M. Yardley

Abuse is a rainbow of colors
Her eyes pink from crying
Her skin white as the blood
drains from her face every time
the door slams.

Bruises blossom on her face, and arms
and hands
and chest
and back
and legs
Even on her feet
And inside her body.
Blue, purple, yellow, green.

He rests his arm around her neck instead of
around her shoulders
And hugs her too hard, leaving red marks
Pressed into her flesh.

But like her body, her smile is also a rainbow
Viridescent cash stashed
in a bag
All of her important papers
The color of milk
Photos of her mother in that beautiful sepia

More bones
may have to break
More unborn babies
may be lost

But when she is ready, so am I
with our matching girlhood star tattoos
She'll slam the mismatched purple door on my blue car
The color of bruises, she always said
Her smile a red slash on her face.

WHY DOESN'T SHE JUST LEAVE?
by Emma Lee

What's hers is his: that's how it works. His is not hers.
He empties her purse, leaves it, like her, lying prone.
His princess bruises easily, not like others.
He checks her emails, social media and phone.

He empties her purse, leaves it, like her, lying prone.
He tops up his wallet with anything valuable.
He checks her emails, social media and phone.
Nothing inappropriate: all predictable.

He tops up his wallet with anything valuable.
She won't leave. He double-checks her phone and cover.
Nothing inappropriate: all predictable.
Nothing from friends, family or a stranger.

She won't leave. He double-checks her phone and cover.
He needs her. She is his. She makes him valuable.
Nothing from friends, family or a stranger.
If she leaves, he'll take his life. She'll be culpable.

He needs her. She is his. She makes him valuable.
His princess bruises easily, not like others.
If she leaves, he'll take his life. She'll be culpable.
What's hers is his: that's how it works. His is not hers.

MY HUSBAND'S HOUSE
by H.V. Patterson

My husband's house wants my bones.

Greedy old house: already full,
grasping after more.
Rafters: stacked tibia and femurs,
chandeliers: cascading arches of ribs and skulls,
unseeing eye sockets flicker with candles

Not just bones.
Scattered through his ancestral home,
I find women in pieces:

Hair threaded into pillowcases
skin in the paint, blood in plaster
fat cushioning antique furniture
muscle layered into bricks
livers, kidneys, viscera
churning beneath the kitchen.
A chorus of frantic hearts beneath floorboards,
trapped souls fluttering, no escape or rest

One thing is missing: lungs.
No moving air in this house,
no voice or breath from those dead women

Six times, I try to leave,
but the path wends into the forest.
Each time, I return, try to keep the peace:
blood, skin, soul—a small sacrifice

A year later, he breaks my arm.
A revelation in pain: I see bone,
my ulna, no longer hidden,
bloody as an ogre's lickerish tooth

I imagine myself dead,
added piecemeal to his house.
To him, I'm a body not yet dismembered,
an Eve waiting to Fall

I scream and find the lungs inside me.
This scream: a thousand women's rage
a banshee's cry for death and resurrection.
Hurricane winds flood the house,
rattle down bones, splinter walls,
uncover thrumming hearts.
A thousand souls flee

In the aftermath, I am alone.
Breath, blood, and bones: I belong only to me

FORECLOSURE
by smeep

It's me.

Did you think I would leave you here
    dying like some mere client?
No, my friend, I'm taking you home with me.

Your house is gone. Well, the good part, anyway.
    Can't you see the cavernous wound in its belly?
Look at the main floor, burned out, blackened, gutted.
    The mortgage is due; the building is lost.
Time to go. Come, I'll walk with you.

I know, I know. You want to stay
    in this exact house. It's important to you.
You hate its curling shingles but love the orange door.
    "That particular shade is so *me*," you say.

Can you even see it through your smoky eyes?
    Look around. You imagine sun shining on white roses
and a basket of fruit in the breakfast nook,
    but the fruit is rotten, the flowers singed.
This kitchen is wrecked, my dear, undone like dinner.

Nothing here to feed the body, my friend.
Let's find something for your soul.

Only attic and basement remain whole; we must climb up or
down.
    We could tidy up the attic or play dirty games in the
    basement.
        So, what'll it be?

Airless attic, mothy red cocktail dresses
    and naked dolls tossed in the steamer trunk
full of yellowed papers,
    where a century of suspended skin flakes
dance with asbestos particles,
    skating new designs onto the deflowered
    curtains,
where toothless dust mites might bite you,
    where the trap door traps you,
where the dry heat roasts you almost to death?

or

Lightless basement, buried underground,
    pipes dripping and furnace growling with hunger,
shit and piss oozing up through the sump,
    mold and must dozing in the displaced swamp,
full of furious creatures scrabbling in the muck,
    where you fumble and fondle in the dark,
where secrets thought drowned threaten to burble into
the light?

No, friend. These rickety ruins cannot shelter you.
    Your wounded soul needs a haven.
Let the fire have this hovel; help me shovel
    this heap of rubble into the ground.

Come, walk with me.
    I'll carry your spade.
At your new home, I promise,
    you will find
waiting for you
    a wicker basket
bursting with fresh oranges.

THE CARVING BLOCK
by V.C. McCabe

Sometimes you're nothing but meat.
—Tori Amos

Apprentice to a butcher, my father was.
The butcher was his father—
like father, like son.
Their wives were so much meat—
beaten tender by fist.
Pawpaw taught Daddy howta
lay 'em down, pound 'em out flat,
cut 'em, gut 'em, string 'em up high—
it's hog heaven hangin' whore hooves,
drawn & quartered, dangling
fresh flesh lanterns on meathooks.
Passover's come early round here,
so paint the doorways
bloody & howl.

METASTASIZE ME
by Tiffany Meuret

The growth on my back, full of sight, blinks uncomfortably as you approach
It sees and sees—that's all it does

Yours is made of teeth and
feeds on pupils as we pass in the hallway, clutching swaths of my skin between their points
as we swipe our bodies together in too close spaces, panicking at our inability to avoid one another

My growth eyes are tired
We want to sleep, for the love of god, stop willing us to speak
Let me keep my visions private
My body is already laid so bare, what the fuck else do you want from me? I don't know
I don't want to know

We watch, we shrug, we process, we remove, we extinguish
And you
You take the bits of us that are left and consider your invoice paid
Soon I'll be blind
I'm not sure if either of us will notice

I THOUGHT THINGS WOULD CHANGE
by Juleigh Howard-Hobson

"...werewolves are born, not made. No matter how many times they bite someone, that person will not turn, though they will probably bleed profusely..."—Molly Harper

The bites might bleed bad, but it's the fractured
bone
that brings the pain. Every chip and shard
is prone
to reminding me of whose fault
they are. Mine.
He never means to assault
me. Ever. Hind
sight is twenty-twenty.
I knew that he hid
a secret from me
about what the moon did
to him, how he
goes berserk when it's full. But
he loves me
and he can't help not being what
I need
him to be all the time. The bite wounds
bleed,
then they heal, like the bone. I hate the moon.

HYSTERIA
by Jude Clee

In the honeymoon suite, I dream of eyes the same shade as
clouds before a storm.
    Like an invisible face hovering over mine
close enough to lick me
(if it wanted to).

A chore chart taped to the fridge comes with a *happy now* from
him.
And I am—
until the dishes glisten in the sink
and *why-didn't-you-just-ask* turns into *quit-nagging-I'm-trying-*
to-relax.

It comes to a head over a week-old container of Pad Thai,
the leftover smell wafting up to my office.
The shredded chore chart sprinkles the kitchen tiles like
snowflakes.
I'm sorry, Babe, but I can't talk to you when you're like this.

He matches my hysteria with the calm of a waveless sea
while I'm left drowning.

The eyes return with a knowing twinkle and a mouth twisting
into a molar-filled smile.
The next morning, fresh red dots bubble on my legs.
I'm starting to think it's not sleep paralysis.

Jacob Hunter arrives in blood and agony
plus my overly active gag reflex thanks to Dear Husband's pizza
box smell.
You don't want me to starve, do you? This is hard for me too.

Dear Husband leaves for the night, while the nurses insist the baby sleep with me
shoved on my naked chest, rooting around fruitlessly.
The eyes gaze down at me in my hospital bed, bright blue against the drab walls.

What do you want from me?!
He needs to eat, the nurse's words are sharp blows.
The eyes don't blink, not even when the teeth sink into my shoulder.
I scream.
The nurses scold me for being difficult.

My toes are a glossy, seafoam green and the house is a warzone:
an upturned cereal bowl sops milk into the rug
the toybox tipped over its treasures,
and Jacob, cranky and crying, sits in a dirty diaper I can smell from the doorway.

Did you just sit on your ass all afternoon?
The controller slams on the hardwood floor.
Jacob wails in my ear, ten baby fingers digging into my skin.
Goddammit!
Why do you always come home and bitch?!
I'm sorry, okay? Let's just forget it.
And we do,
for a while.

I wake to a sharp pain in my side and blue eyes shining in the pre-dawn light.
Dear Husband squats over me
a bullfrog on a log, never blinking.
Not even when he laps at my stomach.

GOSSIP IN SALEM
by Jacqueline West

It starts small, like everything else.
Two heads bowed together, bonnets touching
like two heavy daisies in a field.
Murmurs traveling with the hum of bees,
still light, still distant, in the sunshine.
And then the gradual collection, petal
by petal, drop by drop, sting by sting.

Soon the sound follows you as you walk,
a whisper like the dragging of your own skirts.
And when you turn, of course, there is nothing
to see. Nothing but your neighbors nodding
back at you, their eyes taking in the state
of your linen, the perfect whiteness of your lace.

With time, it gains mass and you gain strength,
used to pulling this weight along
as you bend in the gardens, take a loaf
from the oven, guide a child by the hand
through the narrow streets. You have
other things to do. Other lives to tend.

You will go on as long as you can,
ignoring the burdens that crush your breath
now, the weight that won't let you raise
your head, fill your lungs. You already know
how this will end. How that first dew-soft whisper
was enough. You know how each voice
throws a twig on the fire. You know
how stories pile up, like stones.

FALL VICTIM
by Jeannie Marschall

You know I live alone
My home, my Castle Eden, though
Sadly
Everyone has learned long ago that we are helpless
Thus my self here flagrantly
Means I am wild space up for grabs so you
Next-door stranger
Can just waltz in
Carelessly
Calm as can be
And take from me.

Well, it's true—I am just
Happy little me, friendly and charming
Waving to you as you wave to me as you drive yourself
Home from a long day of work
I made you do it, naturally every smile is
Practically an invitation, isn't it—
isn't. It
wasn't.
We know that.
Yet here you are, trampling my green.

There's a sound in my house, and this my lair
it speaks to me. It has
intimately
surrounded me for so long that we know each other's
rhythms, habits, creaks. This is wrong.

In darkness I slip out of bed, alert, a wake
of fear dragging behind me, but more than that
bristles
along my spine. This. is. mine.
I move
A mirror of eons of ancestresses as I step unknown
As
You
Drive
Yourself
Into my home.

You truly think you can just jar in unchallenged
Rough as you please
Calm as can be
And take from me.

The thing is, the thing is
They
taught
us
wrong.

And now you brought a sneer to a death fight
You set foot in what is mine and now all that is mine is afoot
Rising up ducking down coiling and waiting because
Only a fool steps blind into a space unknown in the night
Oh foolish close-by stranger
Unlike you I grew up darkness-trained a sensing danger she who
has to be

45

Unlike you I absolutely feel when there are eyes on me
A lesson and message recited incessant for
More than a lifetime of always-assessing and mind-glares of
Tales of fatality keeping me making me shaping me
Ready.

It's your own fault, see
Why are you wearing such
Viciously shoved inescapably teetering
Tumble down stairwells and broken bone clothes
When I know so much better
Just where my keep's keeping its
Teeth?

I FEAR FOR HER

by Naching T. Kassa

I fear for her,
This pale woman,
Covering her shame with black glass,
Painting the purple with powder,

The light bleeds from the sky,
Heralding the day's death,
And the arrival of him,
The stranger who lives among us,

I clutch her arm,
As he staggers in,
Surrounded by shadow,
Death brimming in his eye,

Pale woman says nothing,
Avoiding his razor-tongue,
She serves in silence,
A word might mean a wound,

The spirits glide around him,
These demons of the day,
Perching on his shoulder,
Leering in their glee,

Papa! Where have you gone,
Why did you leave her,
To the mercy of Hyde,
And the heart of Hell,

Violence comes so quick,
Like a storm it builds,
And shatters the world,
A blink is all it takes,

There is no love here,
And I can only watch.

LOST YEARS

by H. Grim

Can't breathe,
don't breathe,
you told me not to—

breathe.

Breathe a word of,
what happened
inside our house
(not a home)
never a home,
within those walls.

Mother.

Stewing,
marinating,
inside this—

blood,
my blood,
generations of blood.

They said blood
is what matters,
blood will always
be there for you.

When blood,
your blood,
was what taught me
to hurt,
to feel pain.

Mother!

Kept under
lock and key,
cover up—

Cover up yourself,
your discomfort
unraveling,
like intestines,
those lies that you
covered for him.

You stood by,
in his shadow,
disappearing,
while the brakes
they were cut.

The irony of
you giving me
life—

And then,
slowly,
achingly,
taking the breath
(don't breathe)
from me.

GLASS HOUSE
by Colleen Anderson

I reached out to the light
past the glass
broken vases, broken goblets, broken shards
you had smashed against the wall

Shards embedded in my hand
cutting deep and to the heart

The only heat—my tears falling
on my fingers as they searched
wounds weeping onto glass

The only hurt—my molten pain
glass that flowed into the wound
liquid, moving with my loss

The only glass left unbroken
your glazed anger
wounded—I was left with stones

THE BLOOD ON THEIR HANDS COVERS MY WRATH

by Vanessa Jae

My paper-thin wings
are a challenge to the rough hands
of those who enjoy the thrill
of slicing a stake through my thorax
without the mess of bones
such hangings otherwise bring.
I still breathe
when I hit my head on the lid of a jar
filled with fumes burning my spiracles;
when they squeeze my body
between their fingers, sometimes
too hard, and my viscera explodes
all over them and my beautiful wings,
when they are frozen or soaked
in too much alcohol, lose all vibrancy and
I turn the color of death.
The greatest mistake of their life
was claiming my beauty
for their entertainment,
was failing to recognize the true colors
of my being for what they are:
a promise for revenge.

ELEGY WITH ANGEL OF DEATH, QUICK AS NIGHT AND GLITTER (A GHAZAL, AFTER KLIMT'S "DEATH AND LIFE", FOR C/KR+AH)

by Saba Syed Razvi

His face appeared, a sudden, a spark of fireflies.
But in the garden, girl of blossom and fireflies.

Your body falling like a stone again in my sight,
unexpected as this evening dark, with fireflies.

Mantle of shadows, blues and grays, all ungreened like time,
Your other half blooms like dusk's garden with fireflies.

You held your voice inside a box, like wings, pinned and still,
But darkly it slipped from holes tiny as fireflies.

One against the other is a balance across time,
The maiden of Spring longs winterly for fireflies.

These demons spin like moths, yoked with threads of unspun fate,
Your own demons, quick as the glimmer of fireflies.

A skull beneath the skin, a seed of winter, waiting.
A blush of romance, your eyes ablaze like fireflies.

Your body an echo in this hallway, not now home.
Your body, fled with another flash like fireflies.

The maiden in pinks and violets still feels touch,
Skin soft as wings, as kisses lit, sweet as fireflies.

The ghost of you lingers, your leaving an offering,
A comfort from the darkness, now like the fireflies.

From the gloom beneath the silence grows the fruit of you,
A longing to be bright again like stars, fireflies.

You leave the seedlings to sprout like stars outside of time,
You, still, the silence between flashes of fireflies.

What glimmers with the sun's light casts its shadows behind.
The greedy call of darkness awaits the fireflies.

Time unfolds in memory, lingers in the silence.
We wait for sunset's shadow to catch the fireflies.

You, Breeze of Morning, wonder at the echo of loss,
But the breeze of evening remembers the fireflies.

DAUGHTER IS A BAD RELIGION
by *Lana C. Marilyn*

> "you're probably wondering why i've gathered you all
> here today,
> and the reason is that i don't love your mother anymore
> and i'm moving out"

and then there's my mother with a box of tissues on standby and
you can just see it in her eyes, the record scratch, the freeze frame:
"you wanna know how i ended up in this situation?"

and then there's a vhs tape transition to the day i was born. we
pan out
to see the gurgle of a baby, and her skin already smells like a
dream deferred.

and then we flash forward, to us, catatonic, staring blankly, livid
in the living room.

he doesn't look any of us in the eye, just tiptoes on out, survived
by four girls
tucked into the heart of the others like a bottomless russian doll:
my heart
in your mouth in her lap in my hands. we kill ourselves to sleep
and that's the gist of it.

and then it was tuesday again, like it always is

A CONJURATION
by Mary Rajotte

You would quiet my voice,
then muzzle my mouth.
You would stitch my lips shut
to silence those words forbidden.
You would suppress the tidal waters
ebbing within me, envious of
my ferocity, then punish me
for arousing such covetousness.
You would line my apron pockets
with river-stones, then plunge me
'neath the river flow demanding I swim.
You would bind my wrists,
burden me with obligation,
lay me down hard and make me servile
to your whims, then besmirch me
for being bountiful.
Yet these oppressions cannot quell my vigor
for my resiliency is a tempest provoked.
I suffer your lustful glances
letting them lash like brambles across my skin.
I endure your mouth, puckering against your gnarled lips
and gnashing teeth, only to lick the blood away,
swallowing it with a spoonful of honey and a smile.
These unpleasantries you whisper,
to your wretched temptress, your wanton whore,
I keep for my own, muttering them
later in the dead of night,
sowing them deep in the fetid soil
where they molder and take root.

For weeks, I nurture them, coax and caress them,
spit out your bitterness just to nourish them.
Brazenly, they flourish. They sprout stinging barbs and
weep toxins when I bring the mess together,
letting it steep into a simmering rage.
And when finally you come to my bedchamber,
your hunger rising once more, I greet you there.
With your chin in my hand, I force your mouth open,
spoon down my remedy, a crimson-hued toxin
of berries sweetened with honeyed spittle.
Yet no matter how nourished,
still your scorn surges,
but your rancor, I slough away with ease.
When you shun me for my cunning,
when you smite me for my tenacity,
my seedlings only grow taller when
I summon and stir them,
sing to them an exaltation, a conjuration
for those who come after.

A WOLF UPON A TIME
by Roberta Whitman Hoff

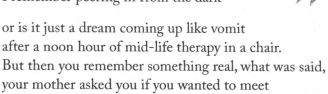

Lucid nightmare: Your mother
the upright wolf skipping in circles
in the lit kitchen waving an old spatula.
I remember peering in from the dark

or is it just a dream coming up like vomit
after a noon hour of mid-life therapy in a chair.
But then you remember something real, what was said,
your mother asked you if you wanted to meet

the big bad wolf. You were terrified.
Yet you were always trying to not to be
afraid, you dreamed of a red cape and basket
full of warm bread and wanted to be a good girl.

So you said yes, you were four years, you walked
hesitantly, your mother frowned, "willful"
she called you, then you saw one of your uncles
in the darkness of the wet woods standing, waiting.

Did mother say, "get closer," nudge you forward
as this big black thing in the leaves came up, huge
and wet, you saw it shaped like a wolf, your heart
pounding, you feel the fear circle into a vortex inside.

It's a grey day out the window, you're supposed to feel
safe in this chair. In the distance your heart is still pounding,
the fear is a vortex, and wolves are warm fuzzy animals,
but who really were those people I'm remembering.

PLAIN WHITE COTTON DRESSES
by Emma J. Gibbon

When they woke up that morning in the mist and green,
in every yard, a plain white cotton dress.
Hanging from a wire coat hanger on the tree, fence, on the
washing line.
Pure and white and cold
and on each dress, a small note pinned
a white square piece of notepaper.
In formal handwriting, in gray-black ink,
two words:
Why not?

When they were distracted,
Each of their daughters stole that dress specifically made for
them.
Put it on and stole away to the river running just beyond their
yards.
They waded into that cold, bright, soothing water.
Each synchronized with the other.
They felt the gooseflesh cleanse their bodies
and lay in the water for their souls to do likewise.
They allowed the river water to wash over them,
inhaled that bright, cruel scent until their lungs were filled,
and down they drifted, the daughters of the town,
to rest in the silt
in their white, white dresses.

TARANTELLA
by L. E. Daniels

Bitten.
She was bitten.
Her husband tells the priest why she's gone mad:
A wolf spider pierced her bare heel in the sun-scorched field as
She cut artichokes—her tooth chipped; the basket tipped; globes
spilled out like heads.
Now, people gather in the waving heat as she twirls and sweats
And slaps their offerings of water to the ground.
Dance the poison out, one veiled crone says,
Or you'll die.
It's unlucky to dance alone, says another.
Musicians emerge to string mandolins with male cicada
aggregations;
A hammered tambourine splits like a lip: a mirror, an omen, an
incantation.
Her sisters join, all bitten—baskets abandoned; bruised thighs
flash; the priest retreats.
Layers of dust burn to ash as stars poke holes in a hot summer
night.
Sisters spin into oblivion as husbands withdraw
And clean sheets billow
Moonlit, on a line.

FAKE SMILE

by Sarah Jane Huntington

At first, honey dripping words, velvet speech spoken with a
golden tongue
Dreams of bright futures, of hot sun-kissed beaches, our children
playing
True smiles, no tricks
We are stardust, you and I
Redemption, salvation, opportunity, happiness
Storm clouds arrived, carrying the darkest of despairs

A jar in the wrong place, a mug out of line
A misspoken word, a mistake, an error
Small things, it was enough, too much for you
Rage, fire, chaos, games of damnation
Cruelty, injustice, the false weigher of invisible sins
A punisher, sharp fists and spiteful thistle words

Weakened, lost, boiling in water that used to be cool
Make-up for bruises, creams to soothe, mind in turmoil
Apologies, promises, a temporary truce
Change, a broken-down train that never arrived
White flags raised in surrender
A merry-go-round, trapped in a circle, a spiral, a descent

False smiles, all tricks
Murder, death, a statistic, a number, one of millions
Fear is the glue that binds
Let the wicked fall, let the guilty suffer
A dying flower, I was born to bloom
Rot lives in your heart, inside your soul

Callous words, cruelty for fun, taunts, laughter
Pain, agony, blinding white-hot terror
Survival, keep breathing, take root
Battered, bloody, is this what I am?
No escape, no exit, no light
Existence is fading, hope is obsolete

Blame, accountability, guilt
You give labels to me, unwanted gifts
Further violence, no apologies spoken
This is how it ends
Fake smiles, all tricks
Dead inside, my body follows

One toxic punch too many
Down I fall, a cascade of solitude
Oblivion welcomes me, wounds and all
You promised to love me
I was supposed to bloom
Instead I wither, life extinguished

GHOST SLUDGE
by Tiffany Morris

We go where
the ghost sludge
seeps through rose-strewn
walls and stairs bleed petals
of dust.

We walk past the shadows
room to room to room
stained with sage, smoke, ember
invocation: filthy eyed &
hand smudged, shearing memory
from its bones,

the day is sterile—
nothing hums here
nothing is shown, nothing
unspooled from the hissing
unholy emptiness
of the halls.

When you brush past me,
an amnesiac afterimage:
locusts give birth
in the dollhouse.

OH, BROTHER
by Elizabeth Stickney Devecchi

Boys will be boys.
    The closet is dark
It's partly my fault.
    Stay deep in the shadows.
I have upset him.
    Hold your breath.
All siblings fight.
    Quiet your sobs.
He cannot help it.
    Swallow the pain.
His anger will pass.
    Don't draw attention.
His footsteps draw closer.
    Close your eyes.
His words grow sharper.
    Cover your ears.
One thought, one goal.
    Survive.
Survive.

THEY EAT THE MOTHER
by Lindsay King-Miller

In spiders of the genus *Stegodyphus*
Maternity is a method of suicide
The mother digests herself to feed her young

The circle of life is a small hungry mouth
A trembling in the silk triggers predatory instinct
She shakes the web, and they come running
All the spiderlings squirming drops of dew
Inherit enzymes to dissolve chitin
Render the mother's body

Imagine the still center of the web
Imagine a daughter's tender fangs
The many-legged beast crawls up my throat
Asks, how much would I give

I fold your small shirts
I sing you lullabies
I clean the crumbs around your lips
I think of spiders

It must feel good
To disturb the web
To ring the blood bell
To call the children home for family dinner
To say the final grace
Their little feet playing hymns
On the strings she wove
It must feel good
To race full speed at the horizon of her own exoskeleton

Isn't there pleasure in the shuddering
Ticking clock of a body
Doing what it's made for
Isn't instinct another word for joy

Of course I envy her the clarity of absorption
Isn't it easier to sacrifice everything at once
Than peel away in pieces
Fold nightmares away with last year's sweaters
Clean gravel from your bloody knees
and tell you when your grandmother dies
Wouldn't I rather you liquefy my heart
And drink it dry in one swallow

Wouldn't I want to go that way
Eyes closing on your well-fed smile
Knowing
For one moment, for one meal
I gave you all you needed

THOSE LAZY SUMMER NIGHTS
by Jessica Peter

The suburb rests, shadows lengthening in
lazy streaks across the pavement.
Late summer sun sets in glorious
cotton candy pink above the bungalows.
These houses are no skulls, there's no
blank-eyed windows, no broken teeth.
It's kids on bikes, golden dogs, and
crickets singing in the grass-scented gloam.

Inside, though.
It's your back to the closet wall,
Pressed in so tight (become one with the clothes, become one,
become one)
And your heart's beating so fast.
And you think he might hear, he might hear the
tha-thump   tha-thump   tha-thump
It's your hands shaking, holding the biggest knife you could find
(It's the best you could do,
given the circumstances,
given this).
Slippery grip, slippery grip.

And it's holding your breath,
Listening for the telling creak of a footstep,
And *telling* yourself lies like:
He'll never find you,
&
You're going to make it out of here alive.
And just knowing, knowing, that deep down knowing
What comes next.

And then it's the creak.
It's the step.
And the final telling.

THE DARKNESS BURNS BRIGHTER ON THE OTHER SIDE

by Cindy O'Quinn

...finding absence of light

No two ways about it—some people were meant to be born hard while others remained soft, and no set match to tackle the beast the world became. Sometimes, being born hard was your only saving grace.

He was his father on the inside. On the outside he looked of no relation to the man whose seed from which he had been spawn. Evil was an inheritance, one received internally, so it was more efficiently hidden from the world.

When he said he loved me to the bone, I found it an odd way of expressing one's love. But that was how he interpreted love… to the bone with the aid of well-sharpened loppers. All ten of my toes were the first to go, then off came my fingers for roasting before he took my nose.

Arms and legs were part of the feast. That's the last I remembered before it was my head that was chopped to feed the beast. But he loved me… to the bone. Every last one until my body was completely gone. Only my soul remained my own.

I woke up six feet under, and there wasn't a string to be found, therefore no chance for me to be saved by the bell. Some graveyards held no markers, so like lint clinging in my pocket, the memory of me would have to be strong enough to hold for a lifetime.

The night was full darkness…

It was an eerie sight, buzzards perched on three old crosses along a dirt road. The crosses weren't atop a hill like most. They stood in a wallow; a hollowed-out space between two hillsides, fit only for feral swine. Hidden and full of shadows made the scene feel all the unkinder.

There were few men, if any, who would admit women held the greatest of titles, therefore making them the strongest of all people. I knew it to be a fact after I clawed my way out of the grave and came eye to eye with the trio of birds.

And the darkness called back to me in the heart of night when I believed in aloneness, only to be proven wrong by the unquiet language of the dead reaching out to me the only way they knew how... by culled cries of sorrow carried on unbroken memories kept real by the ashes of bone.

The price of admission was higher than I expected, but I had been born hard and would have no problem finding the evil man. Landing on his back like a dragon before tearing at his flesh—leaving a gaping hole for the sightseers a view of his twisted spine, blackened with death.

Dead was better. A scary thought held in my mind like a memory—only made me believe it to be the actual truth. I kept his ashes and the three buzzards for company. Darkness always did have a way of closing in around me like a coffin.

...but now it burned brighter

WHERE THE MONSTERS LIVE
by Jo Kaplan

My parents always told me
Stay away from unlighted places:
nighttime alleyways
carport corners
frat house basements ripe with beer and sweat
empty parks
bus stop benches
and tomblike crawlspaces.

They didn't know how I would creep
silent-footed, not to creak the floors
and rouse you, or how I would shrink
from your roar—
how I would make myself a ghost
pattern my skin to match the wallpaper
leave offerings of meat
for the hungry thing that lives in my house.

They didn't know you'd make my bones sing
and my eyes black
that your face was a mask
for an empty pit inhaling my name
roping shadows around my wrists
until I am bled dry, made of tissue paper,
blown back from open windows
into your waiting embrace

my soul with your soul
my flesh with your flesh.

PLEASE, DON'T LOOK AWAY
by Emma E. Murray

I was young, naïve, inexperienced.
Not "young and dumb" but
vulnerable.
He took me under his wing, under his
spell
And I followed him with a bell around my neck,
Melting under his hand,
Lapping up his words like cream.
So when he first took that gentle hand and
Struck me
I took it.
Not a word, only a wide mouth,
spilling open with the busted vessels, clumps and clots
like pomegranate seeds.
I cowered under the weight of his deluge of apologies
His *never again* and *enduring love.*
Twin flames sometimes
burn too hot. Don't you understand?
He stroked me with trite, comforting phrases.
Sometimes passion is too intense to be contained.
Combustible.
I nodded along while I slowly seeped into myself,
imploding,
I changed, steadily becoming someone else with every fist.
Each tirade, a storm of wasps.
Hide my puffy eyes.
My freshly crooked nose contoured back to
doll perfection.
To let him rest easy.

Then came the day
Of hands
unlike any hands before.
The words, the stinging, striking, secret things
(*just between us two*)
A sacred love language of violence.
No, that was over.
The sky turned tornado-green, and his whisper was the wind
whipping in my ear.
Don't you know, I could kill you if I wanted? You are mine
stupid bitch
His hands were snakes, slithering 'round my neck, entwining
constrictors.
I cried under the pressure, not because of impending death,
but because I had lost myself.
A wraith of a woman, invisible in a crowd,
Even with her half-halo bruised eyes and her body tender
as an overripe fruit.
I looked into his eyes and knew
we were wrong.
Both he and I. Always had been.
But it was too late.

A HOUSE UNHAUNTED
by Ai Jiang

They told me it was a haunted house,
but the house was not haunted.

The windows shut when the sun drew near.
The doors slammed closed on the rooms
I wanted to enter, and allowed me to settle
only where I wanted to escape.

The curtains covered my eyes, caressed
my neck—sometimes a little too hard,
sometimes clutching a little too tight,
sometimes leaving violent kisses
I first thought were affection,
wanted to believe was affection,
begged for it to be affection.

There was a room, in the basement,
my husband told me never to enter.
I wondered, if like Bluebeard,
he's had many wives,
would there be many dead bodies,
but there sat something far worse.

In his drunken after dinner stupor,
belly-filled with food I made
while I nibbled his leftovers,
I stole his little key covered in grease
from unwashed fingers and crept down
the stairs to discover a million threads
scattered limp, tangled, gnarly on the ground.
Ones he would wound around every finger,
knuckle, joint while awake, pulling open
and shut the windows, doors, curtains,
making me believe the house, the home
he had created for me was haunted when it wasn't.

BODY ENVY
by Vivian Kasley

I don't blame you. After all, I was once inside.
The muse to our beautiful meat puppet; I pulled the strings.
And then he came around, and then he pulled the strings. SO
many strings.
What I wouldn't do to return to you.
To sink back into our velvety skin, burrow in deep, where it's
warm,
then restart our heart and re-animate our pale-yellow bones,
so we can dance, dance, dance, like we used to.
What I wouldn't give to be the thread again, weaving through
the spongy coils of our brain,
spinning our actions and fueling our thoughts, but, better this
time. SO much better.
He took advantage of us. I took advantage of you.
He hated us. I hated you.
He shamed us. I shamed you.
He abused us. I abused you.
He didn't love us enough. I didn't love you enough.
I want another chance. To make it right between us.
I want to let the ones who loved us, *really* love us. I wanna
fucking love me!
But it's too late. I waited too long.

The gut we ignored is flayed and the cords of our neck are visible, the blood that leaked from both is coagulated and as cold as the kitchen tile.

Our limbs are rigid and our eyes no longer a sparkling vivid green, but a silvery milk.

Parts of our sallow flesh resemble the galaxy; swirls of red, purple, black, and blue.

And I'm fading now, body. I'm nothing but mist now and I'm fading!

I'm sorry, body…I just wanted you to know. I just wanted one more chan—

CELLAR
by Tracy Fahey

in the silence
of your aftermath
i take everything
tainted by you
and stow it
in the cellar

i pull up the trapdoor
seal off

crazy puzzles
of upended furniture
you sat on
books smeared
with your fingerprints
snakeskin clothes
you shed

remake the house
configure it
a nest around me

but sometimes
late at night

the walls echo
the grating of
your key in the lock
I wake from
dreams of ancient arguments
to
whispers of my name

i am safe
unless
i stand on
that old trapdoor
to the cellar

where
your old ghost
still walks

FAREWELL, MY LOVELY
by Stephanie Parent

I Needed a Drink

The night I realized I'd spent ten years
in the wrong house, with the wrong man
changing paint colors and hand-towel patterns
and bedsheets because I could not change
my heart or his—

That night I drank enough wine
to make up for ten sober years

I Needed a Lot of Life Insurance

Because sharp objects lurked in every
drawer and dark corner. The only question:
should destruction aim itself outward or in?

I Needed a Vacation

From the dread dredged up like still water
in a basement, the mildew in our foundation,
the house of lies we'd built crumbling to rot

I Needed a Home in the Country

Because I could not stay in this one, not
now that my husband had shed his false
humanity, bared his teeth, pierced my
neck and clawed my arms

What I Had Was a Coat—

To hide the marks he'd left upon me
shield my tender skin so I might venture out
into the world

—A Hat—

To warm me, shelter me, protect me
from rain and snow. The way he vowed to,
but all his promises were only hollow words

—And a Gun—

His gun, kept unloaded in our bedroom closet
bullets in our bedside table
lying in wait while we made love—
made lies. What's true now
are the marks on my arms, the bullets
sliding into the chamber, the weight
of metal in my palms.

I Put Them On

Coat, hat, gun—my armor, more necessary
inside, where my beastly husband sleeps.
I faced his bed, the betraying blankets.
Aimed the gun, imagined pulling the trigger.
Blasting out his long, lolling tongue (the better
to eat you with, my dear).

And Went Out of the Room

I did not need to destroy him; this rotting building
and his own hunger would finish the job.
I took my husband's coat, his hat, his weapon.
For the last time, I left the house that was
no longer our home.

A WOMAN POSSESSED
by Amanda M. Blake

In an ornate chair
Bound and burdened by
Bejeweled brocade
And a golden chain strung
Around a slim neck
A woman
Possessed
By a man

In an oppressively draped bed
The master covers her
With heavy body
Greedy mouth
And grasping hands
A woman
Possessed
By right

Fabric torn in ribboned shreds
From the knife concealed in stays
Blood drips from the body
Smeared mouth
And clawed hands
A woman
Possessed
By invocation

ON ICE
by PS Cottier

There's a gurgling from inside,
the cold white box singing,
chuckling, but she only catches
the occasional word—
snare or *rope* or *dumb*
though sometimes she'd swear
she hears it lisp *asylum*.
Tapping, and clapping too,
as if ten thousand fingers
and two thousand palms
dwelt in the refrigerator,
immune to frostbite and rot.
She awakes, mouses her way
to the murmuring, slapping kitchen,
swings open the heavy door
to a blinding, silent nothing.
She removes the shelves,
squeezes her body inside.
Sings herself a lullaby.
Claps out a childhood game.

PUBLIC HOUSING
by Sarah Yasin

In the ill-lit stairwell
I calculate words.

The hallway door
to my father's apartment
is totally gross.

Washrag nor Clorox wipe meet its knob never.

Its abstinence from hygiene is heroic.

A film of dust and ineffable jelly
sweep the surface of cream painted wood:
a dingy *trompe l'oeil*,
a cesspool map.

The upper edge is stained
by a climbing vine of smudges,
a fingerpaint orgy in brown.

Down the eastern panel
a crack gives way to chipped paint
and grayed wood long neglected.

The door to my father's apartment is a dirty snowbank,
a door once white with symmetric mullions
forming a perfect inverted cross, a heavy metal
band insignia, an upright block-stencil sword.

Cigar incense seeps
down the door's crack
and out beneath the base
telling me he's home,
telling me I'm in for it.

I reach for a match, clench a filter with my teeth.
Glove–free, I fondle the knob.

The decrepit slab bounces shut
behind me.

NIGHTSHADE
by Kay Hanifen

I swallow my words like belladonna
Bittersweet berries the color of bruises
Burning, biting, bubbling in my gorge
Begging to be vomited out
The poison purged by my rage

But his poison was never a lethal dose
It trickled slowly into every word
And then every blow
A subtle weakening of my defenses
That I mistook for growing immunity

I misidentified his lovely flowering soul
As separate from the poison fruit
Something that can be pruned
Snipped away, leaving only flowers
But one cannot exist without the other

The same plant that produces purple flowers
Also births the belladonna berries
The poison is in his roots, his stems, his leaves
And the flowers I fell in love with.

There are some ways to remove a weed
You can burn it, watching the fire purge the sin
You can rip it out at the roots, starving it
Or you can poison the poisoner

A little herbicide in his coffee
And he'll wither away to a brittle husk

METHODOLOGY: INNER CHILD MERCY MASSACRE

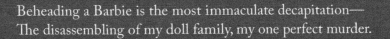
by Ava Serra

Beheading a Barbie is the most immaculate decapitation—
The disassembling of my doll family, my one perfect murder.

Age six or seven—
Somewhere in the time-blur of all ages before eleven—

I kneeled beside the dark ocean of my bed, dragged
My plastic, pink box from its sideways chasm, ready to fill a
morgue.

Pinched the soft PVC of a blonde doll's face—
Watched her ugly.

Hooked two fingers under her skyscraper-sharp jawline and
tugged—
Spinal snap, and forever flawless even in two perfect pieces.

That previous incarnation of me tugged and tugged
Until she had a symphony of hollow *pop*s, an overfilled graveyard.

Some parts she rearranged—ballooned heads hung
On small bodies, two left feet, mismatching skin—

A low-stakes chain of mutations in plastic genes,
A young Frankenstein trying to fashion their breakthrough
experiment

Into a mirror image of their own monster.
But, in the end, no body bore a head,

And child-me buried the beheaded corpses in blushing taffeta,
Gathered the unblinking eyes like flower petals,

Lit a sugar cookie candle, made it a cauldron of hot wax.
Mixing the heads in, the plastic and paint boiling, the ceremony
began

With the same words that drove her to that immaculate mercy-
killing:
This is for your own good.

This will keep you safe, she said, believing safety
To be the exposed, festering skin and nerve in a third-degree
burn.

The left index finger of my six- or seven-year-old self swirled the
synthetic skulls
Into a wax stew, heat gnawing at flesh the same way a flame eats
a page.

When heat met wax met liquid plastic met bone, I locked the
morgue,
Took the candle and its contents, upturned it over my own head,

Murmuring, *This is for your own good. This will keep you safe.*
Sweet inner child mercy massacre.

NOTHING WAS SPARED
by Sophie Kearing

bone
like china, fine and delicate,
reduced to shards on linoleum.
From the ceiling, I stare at my own remains:
an oxidizing stew of crimson and brown
punctuated by tender slices of my wrecked flesh.
bits of me peppering the wall,
obscene against the stark white surface.
Nothing was spared; my demise was thorough…
yet merciful in its totality,
for my sorrows no longer gnash at me
with jagged, yellow teeth,
and my pain has been obliterated…
it has nothing on which to cling.
gray matter reduced to fatless morsels—
vertebrae emancipated from staunch in-betweenness—
femurs bristling with sinew and liberty:
Unanchored. Without function.
Free.

LOVE LETTERS FOR KIRSTY COTTON AFTER 'HELLRAISER' (1987)
by Mim Murrells

Kirsty, did you want it? Did you want them?

Kirsty, did that room make you feel like a kid again? Were you ever anything but a kid? How old even *were* you?

Kirsty, how did the fingers feel in your mouth? Did it hurt? Did it thrill?

Kirsty, is there anything better than the way you feel after the second glass of wine? Doesn't it just feel like the weight of spun glass behind your eyelids? Doesn't love just teeter on the tip of your tongue? Don't all those eyes feel so warm on your back when you leave the room?

Kirsty, I've never blamed you for taking so long to realise.

Kirsty, you dress like a girl-child playing pirates. The trick that boy did with his cigarette wasn't cool enough to warrant a kiss. But that's life for you. A boy can be in your house and he can kiss you. Maybe there was even a little want. There must have been. Why would you have let him do it, otherwise?

Kirsty, do you miss your mother? Did you miss her when he kissed you?

Did you ever get strange looks for calling your father daddy? I think they liked even the *idea* of mine more than they liked *me*, even though he would have hit them if I'd let him.

Kirsty, did you miss your daddy, when you saw Frank behind his eyes?

Kirsty, how does one become underappreciated in their own story? Actually, I can answer that one: everyone is amused by a heinous bitch, but a girl who cries is just uncomfortable to deal with.

Kirsty, did he do it? You can tell me. I miss practical effects. When you could praise their grotesquery and their beauty without praising the fact that they were being used at all. I wasn't there for it, obviously, but it's not like you were either.

Kirsty, were you a child? Was I? I was ugly for the first time in my life. No child is ugly.

Kirsty, did you ever walk into the kitchen to see him sitting there? Did it ever feel like he was lying in wait? Kirsty, did he ever summon you? Did the call come from inside the house?

Kirsty, can you remember how the hands felt on you? Pain doesn't have to touch you. You know what I mean? Jesus didn't cry because he tripped over Lazarus' hearth and banged his shin on the front step. You understand?

Kirsty, do I understand? I love you. I think I understand.

GAIA CREATED
by EV Knight

Burn my body, she said,
When I am gone.
Don't let them see the pain tattooed on bruised flesh
What you did—what I endured
In weakness and self-loathing
Promises made to death-stilled hearts don't keep
Thus, six feet of cold, damp darkness covered her
Grave worms burrowed beneath buttered flesh, feasting on a
tapioca of clots
Beetle pincers mined under nails, affixed them as wings to their
backs
Gnawing away at the virgin flesh—such sweet, honeyed
untouched innocence
Time passed, vermin fed, fatted and strong
Blanketed by a skin freed of secrets
Once more animated by the feast of the living upon the dead
In the moonlit night, the revenant rose
Carried forward by larval locomotion
Writhing, waxen, want
A hunger for the hated
Promise breaker

Sightless eyes, globes of silken nurseries filled with hungry babes
Born of death, seeking the same
Her body found him. Modus unchanged
Except the screams this night belonged to him as their offspring
poured
From her sockets, her sinuses, her cavities
To fill his own.
And Gaia returned
To the earth.

SPEECHLESS
by Nicole Kurtz

My voice grinds on the ears,
On the fragile and weak,
With their long vowels and clipped ends.

My voice crunches on those egos,
And punctures the blown up and puffy privilege
And swollen bags of pride.

Yet, they remain.
Like ivory kudzu spreading and sprawling.
Blanketing my output, stimming my growth,
choking me to silence.

My hands are scraped and scarred
From clearing out
My throat.

PRISON OF VINES
by Abi Marie Palmer

Winding tendrils, ivy teeming
Through the gaping windows,
Down the chimneys crumbling, choking,
Burying the home, the prison, you fled,
Mist-cloaked, fifty years ago.

Still, decrepit, worn, it rises,
That behemoth mired in secrets,
Swamped with stories seeping
Through the ceiling, sporing fitful
Plum-dark shadows on the walls.
Through the floorboards, sanguine shoots
Protrude like twisted fingers of the
Captives flailing haplessly for freedom.

Footsteps. Creaking, trudging, nearing.
Echoes of the creature, the jailor,
Who kept you here, half a lifetime since.
Now, concealed, imprisoned in these walls,
It's waited, growing, festering with hatred.
Monkshood, foxglove, poison hemlock
Running through its lethal veins.
Wheels of fate compel you to its lair
Again, to save your stolen daughter,
Drawn by that same fate that binds
Your bloodline to this wretched place.

Up the curving staircase, clawing
Through the vines that guard the way,
Find the chamber where it keeps its victims,

Steeped in nectar, specimens for ancient rites,
Afloat in nightmares, numb, lethargic.
They can only wait until the ghastly sacrifice.

Breathlessly, you reach the sanctum.
There she lies, suspended in the soporific pool.
All around, the room pulsates with listening leaves.
They quiver. Fungus edges nearer, sensing, scenting an intruder.
Then, the rumbling roar.

It looms in the doorway, hideous and vengeful,
Face of thorns and nettles, mildewed, haggard
Like the day it drew you in before.
Stumbling, you scarper like the clumsy girl
You were the last time. Tangled vines pursue,
A pandemonium of rustling serpents, clasping,
Grasping, swaddling your shaking form.

Naïve to hope you could be disentangled
From your bloodline's endless fate.
Now you join your wayward daughter,
Self-same runaways, you drifted
Down this ancient stream towards
Your final prison, drowned in sleep.

IT WASN'T THE DARKNESS
by Shannon E. Stephan

It wasn't the darkness—bulbs
Flickering free from energy,
Leaving me in sacred solitude.
No, I had been alone before.
The ceiling fan formed a cross of sorts,
A haunting hope of Heaven, born
Of bloody nails and baptisms above the bed.
Is this what it will look like after death?
This sleeplessness, this nothingness,
This barbaric black?

It wasn't the darkness—shadows
Squeezing through window slits,
Laurel limbs scrawling scripture on the wall.
Pointing. Always pointing.
At me because how dare I ask a question?
Did the Virgin Mary play with dolls?
Did she dare to dream?
Did she feel she was being watched, too,
In the manger, in her sleep?

Or did she know it was all a lie?
So she curled, like the fetal Christ,
Balled up by submission, soundlessly
Accepting a sainthood fate,
When really, she was probably raped.

It wasn't the darkness—a steamed
Communion dress and patent leather shoes
Brooding behind closet doors,
Or grandparents who would come with their camcorders.
It was the Sunday morning mass melting
In a priest's mouth:
Threats made of chocolate chips.
And how the confessional always closes in—
Just like this.

It was never the darkness—lying
Awake praying the rosary.
It was asking silently:
But what about Mary?
What about me?

HER BRAVEST DAY
by Louise Worthington

Knees branded by scratches, carpet burns, bruises, and paper cuts from forgotten anniversaries—heal with new, tender skin.

Dressed, you'd never know middle-aged Sharon had been in love before, save for that pink scar tissue on the right knee and her left thigh like crinkled candy paper.

At forty-nine, after eighteen years of marriage, there's a deep marriage line cut into the palm of her hand. Marriage is a dam in the river starting with paper, then silk, ivory, crystal, and bronze. They have built a nest together in this house of theirs.

Once she fell for him. Not from the sky, a branch, a wing, or a stunt from a burning building. Falling in love with him was cooling rain, dripping and dousing, then a drifting mist. Next, snow—icicles, snow angels, snowmen. Strange shapes sculpted from something fallen from the sky. Unfathomable things she hadn't thought possible.

As she stirs the Bolognese, her heart is bubbling. Not with excitement at his return from work. She hides. The searchlight of his voice shines into each room.

He wanted sausages and mash. With gravy. She'd got it wrong. Again.

A stranger is ransacking the house. Attacking her face, kicking her lower back. Under his blue-veined eyelids, there should be a wide corridor where guilt is hiding.

In the taxi to the hospital, the night dark-bellied and grumbling, she touches her face. A warm, ordinary cheek that was his to stroke and kiss. She is a cherry tree blossoming in the wrong season. Her branches sway with each stab of pain and drip of blood. Beside her on the back seat, a trail of cherry blossom, pink-soft petals mid-air, astray. They collect in the footwell of the car.

Beside her is a carrier bag of all the anniversary gifts: the paper, the furniture, the porcelain—a swag of nothingness to him, after all: the twigs and priceless bits their nest was made from which she's polished, dusted, coveted. The gold band on her wedding finger can join them.

The taxi driver reminds her of how he drives with one arm on the steering wheel, the bend of his elbow on the door, and the open window cracked. He once made her a mixed tape they listened to while driving, made plans for their honeymoon, plans brighter than the headlights. But she finally hears the crunch of metal and the smell of a smoking engine.

This time she isn't going to the hospital in a body bag.

She arrives at the hospital stripped of blossom, pale as a skull, leaking sap. A scalpel in her other hand, ready to cut out the marriage line forever.

As she staggers through the doors, faces swim in and out of her vision. Opening her mouth to scream for help, she places one hand centrally on the car horn. Pushes. Leaves it there until it's safe to stop.

ON THE GLASS RIM
by Alyson Faye

Then—

I looked for you—
in car parks
in corridors
in shopping malls,

whilst I danced,
wretched, to your tune,
my fleshy petals,
uprooted, bled…

you were there

Through all the evenings'
languorous lullings,
into valium valleys
riding champagne highs.

you were there

I listened for your steps,
waited for your breath,
your fingertips upon
my thin, fine skin,

whilst I trod water
succumbing to the promise,
to the erotic embrace,
to the kiss trace
and the taste of tears,

you were there

Now—

I look for you—
in my apartment
in mirrors
inside my head

and…

you are no longer there
or anywhere.
We are done.

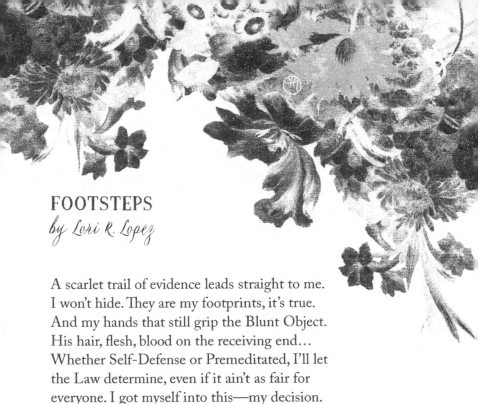

FOOTSTEPS
by Lori R. Lopez

A scarlet trail of evidence leads straight to me.
I won't hide. They are my footprints, it's true.
And my hands that still grip the Blunt Object.
His hair, flesh, blood on the receiving end…
Whether Self-Defense or Premeditated, I'll let
the Law determine, even if it ain't as fair for
everyone. I got myself into this—my decision.

She told me to go and not look back. Told me
countless times. How could I abandon my mom?
Trapped in that bed. He took away her escape.

I never followed in someone else's footsteps…
Always thought for myself. "You're stronger than
any of us," Mama praised. "And plenty stubborn."
Not like her. Afraid of her own breath. Gasping
or stifled—rushing out in huffs—tense and
anxious. Scared. Mostly that my dad would be
home. Iron-fisted. Trudging hard, in a foul mood.

Stamping loudly through the door. His giant Ego
ever-present, overpowering, ominous, unbearable.
Even when he was gone. We loathed his presence.

She hissed, "He'll be here any minute!" I used to
blame my mother for being weak. Then learned
through snippets he would grumble, how she oughta
regret raising a fist to him, talking back—my dad
put her in the chair on wheels. Raydene stood up
to an abusive Bully. Ma wasn't that big, but she
let him have it. Gave him a Shiner, a crooked nose.

To keep him away from me! One night, Del folded
that chair, hauled it out, threw it in the bed of his
truck. We never saw the thing again. He sold it.

And wouldn't let her visit a doctor anymore…
No matter how much she hurt, she'd smile at me.
"Hush now. I need you to nevermind. It's okay.
You've gotta stay safe, baby girl, for both of us."
Whispers brimming with pain and fear. "Don't do
anything, Jess, promise." I tried and tried to keep
that pledge. Until I couldn't. It was time…

The steps across the floor were bare and light.
Unnoticed, unheard, unhurried, unfeared, until
it was too late. I was already right behind him.

We lived in that house, under his rule, for ages.
I always knew I had his rage, his temper, deep
in my core. Like a Protection Spell, a Talisman.
Not for me. I would use it for her. When things
got really bad. I guess I had some of her restraint,
her gentle spirit, because I waited so very long…
My daddy's eyes and anger. Mama's soft tread.

Back when she could walk. The damp footprints
of fetching a crowbar in the rain faded. The wet
crimson tracks endure. My footsteps. All mine.

BURN IT DOWN
by Christina Ladd

Third down the street on the left
Old brown house
A little overgrown,
But as they say
Strong bones

I will drill holes in my own strong bones
To fill them with fire
I will pluck out my eyes
And set the sockets with flint
So that when I scrape my gaze
Over this place
It will catch.

Do you know what twenty years of fear
Will do to a person?
It's twenty years of
Running water on a marble statue
Wearing me away

No more.

The glaciers have fled,
The rainforests have burned,
Everything bows in the end
To fire.
Even the gods feared
What we would do with it
And what I am confronting
Is so much less
Than a god.

I might be a god
The god of heat
And light
The god of the first curl of smoke
Like a baby's finger
Gripping your own
New life from old patterns
To defy
—not a house—not a home—
But a heap of dry bones

'Shall these
Bones live?'
No, but I shall
Live
I shall
Burn
With living

CEASING TO BE
by Patricia Gomes

Trembling, her skinny pale legs
marched her six-year-old self
to her Godmother's kitchen,
which would be safe,
which would be loving,
which would be healing
because how could it not
be?
In that very cozy kitchen,
just last week,
Godmother presented her with a gift,
pink boxed and silver tissue-wrapped,
to wear for First Communion.

A genuine white rabbit fur stole!
She had never owned anything so lovely,
so dainty,
so grown-up feminine before.

The Godmother bent low
so this child, this shaking child
could whisper in her ear
of what the uncle,
the beloved of the Godmother,
did
to this reed of a tiny being
in the cellar of this cozy house.
Where he touched her,
how he touched her,
where he made her touch him

and Oh!—how she hated the smell of him.
The Godmother nodded, then shooed her out.
Everything would be fine again,
she just knew it!

And it was.

Godmother sent for the stole.
Ma gave it back,
and neither Godmother nor Uncle
ever spoke to her again.

NIGHT'S MARE
by Marisca Pichette

two legs—me
three legs—table
four legs—chair
six legs—bed
eight legs—the thing beneath.

eight, twelve, twenty
too many to count
clinging, crawling
claws like fingernails—
like lust.

mouths unseen, I hear
saliva soaking into
scratched and bruised
imperfectly varnished floors.

uncountable legs cover
bed, chair, table.

uncountable mouths cover
me.

AND NO WAY TO WALK AWAY
by Amanda Hard

Among these Harper Valley PTA mothers, you are
already found *Guilty*. When whispers call you

co-conspirator, you have no defense. Yet you are
not just the woman with darkness under her eyes,

Dollar Store makeup carefully applied to conceal
shame as well as bruising. You are *Mother*, more

than woman, this monumental role: Life-giver.
Heavy hangs the head that wears the macaroni necklace.

Mother—the organizing principle of family,
life-preserver, life-protector. Yet who protects you

against bruises the shape of child-sized fingers,
bite marks from baby molars, a tangerine-sized fist

slammed into the soft hollow of your throat? None
to witness Man-sized fury in Pokemon pajamas.

"*Leave him*," they counsel. Sew him into sheets
doused with oil, set ablaze. Or lie next to him,
Burn for your sins, your choices, dear "*mother*,"
sleeping with the Enemy out of ease, out of fear.

"*Leave the man. You have the child to think of.*"

What they don't [want to] know is that you sleep
alone, bedroom door locked tight between you,
a barrier of wood and brass and unlikely prayer,

(Clicked) not against monsters in monster form,
(Latched) not against monsters in husband form,
(Deadbolt thrown) to keep out a monster with your

face, your genes: your father's flying fists, grandpa's
rage, your brother's hand punching holes like those
small ones you've repaired in countless rented walls.

Asleep, he is only nine years of little boy. At birth,
little more than five fragile pounds. *Your eyes*

they said. *He has your eyes*, which means exactly
what? Swollen from crying? Lowered in shame?

Disturbing, the way demons can't be exorcised.
Despairing, a mother who fears her own child.

ANNIVERSARY
by Alison Bainbridge

We're wilting at this table. Placed here,
gilded and pretending to be alive
as we shed parts of ourselves into the gulf;
deep bruises between untouched plates.
Arterial dark. The slow patter of their descent
drowns out the sound of your breathing.
We repeat old arguments in silence;
hatred rich and heady as the smell
of dying roses; as the taste of blood
from the split lip you gave me, and the almond-tang
of poisoned wine.

BLOOM
by Jessica Sabo

She grows in the dark,
requires prolonged periods of
fragmented
habitat to thrive.
In eight weeks, her legs are
hearty red:
she is the meal of an apple;
a marriage of exposure.
She feasts on nothing; is
naked, scraping just
enough from the gut
to grow herself strong like
the need to survive
this
is more than hers
alone.
In a last-attempt conservation effort,
she drenches herself in summer sun
and in
fall, she decays in
darkened corners, windowless rooms,
crawlspaces, in between
calloused palms—
all the places where colors fade.

AT THE CANNIBAL'S FUNERAL
by E.F. Schraeder

No one arrived to share her grief,
so the widow stood alone,
recalling the dank graveyard
of their basement. Those finger bones—

how she screamed at that first discovery.
Hands wrung, her eyes averted.
This secret could kill me, she thought,
but neither of them went hungry.

A life is a life, he said. And yet—
Sometimes sorrows shrivel
when held too long in the light.
What does it mean

to miss a monster?
To miss his mean heart
or those calloused, carving hands.
A crooked smile pinched her face

as she stood at the open casket.
She placed a single white rose on his chest,
a symbol of purity to bury with him.
She rubbed the smooth, pearled buttons of his shirt.

In her purse she hid a small clear bag
filled with clipped nails and hair.
That's what's left of him now.
Something small enough to swallow.

DON'T LOOK NOW
by Linda Kay Hardie

*Sticks and stones may break my bones
But words will hurt forever.*

She slaps the kid across the face. "Shut
up," she snaps, and raises a hand to hit
again. The child's howl quiets to a whimper, face
red where mom's palm landed. The woman

turns back to the grocery shelf,
and the child, with a furtive look, grabs
cookies. He rips open the box, hoping
to avoid notice. Mom turns and

shrieks, "Stupid fuck, just like your father, you
never listen," and hits again. The child wails
louder than before, and shoppers pass by, eyes
averted, pretending not to see, while I

stand transfixed, transported back in time—
I never cried, but then, he never
hit me, not with his fists anyway. He
knocked me down with words, which are

harder than fists and more insidious.
He could beat me in public with a few quiet
well-chosen words and no one
even had to pretend not to notice.

CLICK HERE TO DEFINE
by Emily Vieweg

Rape.
 Noun.
 Definition of *rape*—entry one of four.
  1. unlawful sexual activity
   But only if you're not asking for it—
   with short skirts or
   flannel shirts or
   keds or
   smiles or
   frowns or
   saddle oxfords.
      Count the ceiling tiles.
      Two Four Six Eight Ten Eleven.
      By two four six eight nine.
      Eleven by nine.
      Nine by eleven.
      Eleven by nine.
      Nine times nine is eighty-one.
      Eighty-one divided by three is
      Twenty-seven divided by three is
      Nine.
      Nine by eleven
      to the water cooler outside the dorm room
      down the hall around the corner
      ten steps to the door
      to the hall
      to the stairs
      to the door
      to the stairs
      to the outside air
  2. an outrageous violation <u>Click here to define.</u>

violation. noun.

The act of violating: the state of being violated: such as

  a. infringement, transgression, <u>click here to define</u>

      specifically: an infringement of rules in sports less serious
than a foul and usually involves technicalities of play

  b. an act of irreverence or desecration: profanation.
<u>Click here to define.</u>

  c. disturbance, interruption click here to define

  d. rape entry 1 sense 1, ravishment.

      <u>Click here to define.</u>

Rape.

  Noun.

  Definition of *rape*—entry one of four.

  1. unlawful sexual activity carried out forcibly or under threat of injury

      just say no

      means yes

      means

      she asked for it

      he said

      she said

      he says

      she said

      tes

      no

      yes

      no

      no

      no

  2. an outrageous violation <u>Click here to define.</u>

  3. an act or instance of robbing or carrying a person by force—

      The bride is carried across the threshold

      after her father gives her away

      the dowry a payment of business.

  Verb. raped; raping.

  Definition of *rape*—entry two of four.

    Transitive verb. <u>Click here to define.</u>

A verb that requires an object to receive the action.

1. to commit rape on
    to commit "unlawful sexual activity" on
    to commit "an outrageous violation" on
    to commit "an act or instance or robbing or carrying a person by force" on

2. a. Despoil—Click here to define.
    despoil. verb.
    > To strip of belongings, possessions, or value. Click here to define.

    > value. noun.
    > 1. Monetary worth of something. Market Price. Click here to define.

    Back Click

    Back Click

2.a. Despoil.

2.b. *archaic* Click here to define.

> *In this dictionary the label archaic is affixed to words and senses relatively common in earlier times but infrequently used in present-day English.*

Back Click

To seize and take away by force. Click here to define.
Force.
> Noun.
> 1.a.1. strength or energy exerted or brought to bear: cause of motion or change: active power
> 1.a.2. *capitalized*—Used with a number to indicate the strength of the wind according to the Beaufort scale.
> 1.b. moral or mental strength
> 1.c. capacity to persuade or convince

2.a. military strength
2.b.1. a body (as of troops or ships) assigned to a military purpose

> What about my body
> Is my body your force to reckon

2.b.2. forces *plural*: the whole military strength (as of a nation)
2.c. a body of persons or things available for a particular end

> My body is a person
> my person is a body
> my person is more than a body

2.d. an individual or group having the power of effective action
2.e. *often capitalized*: POLICE FORCE. usually used with the italics *the* Click here to define.

3. violence, compulsion, or constraint exerted upon or against a person or thing.

Back Click.

2.a. Despoil.
2.b. *archaic* Click here to define.

Other words from *rape*
Verb
raper   there is no link to click to define.

Synonyms for rape
Synonyms: Verb
Assault click here to define
Force click here to define
Ravish click here to define
Violate click here to define

Visit the thesaurus for more.

HORROR, IDENTIFIED
by Lynne Sargent

It is not about the lights going out.

It is about not being able
to turn them back on

without a blessing,
without a little luck.

And if time restarts?
the microwave clicks back on
the dawn returns,

the fable of infallible eternity
does not.

AUGURY
by Belicia Rhea

Your vampiric gaze spells the herd
enamored by that sagging charade,
tar-black saccharine eyes,
those fists and talons scrape bloody.
Smoke clears and you're a reversed card,
two faces of the idiot fool.
I'm slurping bottom of the bowl,
still freezing as bumps crawl up my thighs.

You gleam, nursing your glory of filth
and I wonder if you find it absurd
that these maggots feast upon you too.

We are parked outside of your house at sunrise.
Hollow-points still aimed for my guts
that I can never seem to find in these moments.
I note silence, sleeplessness of lost factory sheep.
You grip my bruised-up neck and
my hands a constant trembling   shake the earth

in the bleak light upon emerging dawn,
a lone blackbird sits atop a wire
as if to tell me something.

PANDEMIC APARTMENT SOUNDS
by Larina Warnock

It's best these doors remain hidden
else cracks that spiderweb through
stairwells, that house wells of spider's
webs, draw the attention of inhabitants
on floors below and floors above.

The man on 3 calls it love when he
raises a bottle to his lips. His wife knows
his kiss will be too hard tonight, spittle
dripping between them like the secret
that she wishes he might cough, just

a little, just enough to justify asking
her daughter's best friend's mother
if the girl can wait this out with her
on the first floor, but that other mother
knocks on the door on 2 daily to check

whether the elderly grocery checker
with COPD is okay. These days, everyone
is in everyone's business, and while the
guy on 2 probably knew all these years
what was happening, he just couldn't climb

another floor. The woman on 4 is sure
to notice now that everyone's home, but
calls to police for domestic disturbance
may or may not be appropriate.
Eventually they will run out of liquor.

Meanwhile, this wife wonders whether
sounds of violence can carry through the cracks
to the daughter and her friends at ground
level, whether the beveled edges of the stairs
are pointing up or down.

I SEE
by L. Marie Wood

I see blue skies with cotton ball clouds hanging over my head
ready to dump the rain they carry onto me.
I see pineapples on the vine
Pumpkin roots crawling, spreading,
invading
permeating
dominating
waiting.
Blood oranges pinpricked, crying thick, sappy tears for me to see.
And
I
see flowers with hair for petals,
eyes that roll in sockets too weak to hold them still.
Flies land on the lidless things, bite at the flesh, dip their feet
in the carnage, let it soak in deep, and then rub them together.
I see want on her lips,
blood red and foul,
smelling of waste and false promises.
Wipe it away
Smear it like so much lipstick drawing on pale cheeks.
A crayon on canvas.
Lick the juice from the pocked skin, bitter and sweet to trick
the senses

Bittersweet like wool on a summer's day
to mislead the mob
to fool the fool.
I see orange light under a black sky and bite my lip
make it bleed
to pay for passage.

CONSUMPTION
by Harley Woods

She is so beautiful I want to drown...
Edge and line juts perfectly,
cutting the liquid love around her.
But her curves, oh, her curves.
I watch them swirl around,
and stir the pour where she's submerged.
Her body turns like a yolk, mixing into
this bath of lavender soap.

I want to be closer. I want to drink in
the spilling beauty that I can only
admire from here. I wish I was the water.
I wish I was the light glinting
on the smooth, polished skin
that she drapes in the basin.

Even the way she becomes alert,
much like a doe seeking her hunter,
entraps me in her poised body.
The potion drips down her lines and
stains the crevices she tries so desperately
to hide. Each droplet itself seems placed so
divinely, as if Aphrodite could see that
she, here before me, is too heavenly
to allow to breathe. As if she had
stepped outside a painting
where an artist let her come to be.

My forehead touches the glass. It
bluntly exudes a sound.
I exhale, and the fogged pane covers my smirk.
No one will ever live up to this,
this magnificent creature unwilling
to flee. And I love her for it.
She is so beautiful I want to drown… her.

CHILDHOOD MAGIC
by Victorya Chase

We picked lilacs from Mrs. Stomp's yard, hiding
The deep purples and soft lavender around our room

A secret charm; a warding spell
Yarn became a spider's web covering

The doorway in intricate designs of protection
Security that forgot the existence of scissors

Leaves were wishes and we scratched secret maps into bark
Childhood magic was supposed to be strong

But ours never worked. I hid under the bed
The wire frame above a patchwork of thorny thickets.

I heard my mother, each step anger intensifying
my bruises, flowers fading and new, remembering

Her heavy hand. I closed my eyes,
safe in the dream of a spindle prick.

DESECRATED
by Raina Allen

she says i've been defiled
by the bloodletting.
confinement with a midwife
who sees me unclean
and rinses my newborn son with hose water.

i have been made impure,
torn on perforated lines
like notebook paper.
and my love slides letters underneath the door,
but will not touch my cheek.

spoiled milk in leaky pipes
dribbles on my blouse.
veiled confessions spoken through tears,
but all these stains wash away—
all but one:

the rapine of my only home
and the muddied welcome mat
under a flickering porch light.
i can not let you in;
i don't live here.

YOU CAN ALWAYS TELL A BARKER GIRL
by Victoria Nations

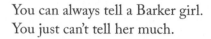

You can always tell a Barker girl.
You just can't tell her much.

You can tell a Barker girl that women who get beat are weak.
You can tell her as her mother,
her aunt, her girl cousin.
You can tell a Barker girl that a beaten woman brought it on herself,
even if you're at the family potluck with a black eye
or a bruised neck.
You can tell her she's a dumb bitch if she lets her man do it.
You can tell her even if you're a beaten woman yourself.

You can't tell a Barker girl why beatings are private.
You can't tell her how you screamed on the kitchen floor,
as the cousin she looks up to, as the aunt who tells her saucy secrets,
as her mother who's supposed to protect her.
You can't tell her how you grabbed the knife from the counter.
You can't tell her if you were going to stab yourself
or your man towering over you.
You can't tell her when a dumb bitch doesn't know herself.

THE FOXHOLE PANTRY
by D.C. Houston

The madness lies midway,
the pale, between the dawn and the midnight, of his rage.
Surrendered, parry long eclipsed.
Rolling darkness, ice, in your collapsing veins.
You arc unbound.
By gravity, by life.
A drifting raven, your dissociative way,
save for the noisy static, of your own orbit. This temporary lull,
a foxhole,
you greedily scamper through.
The hot iron press, the tunnel,
where ringing isn't the shattering of tiny, broken, things.
Moments of lucidity, archaic blinks,
what living, could be, in the absence of this, malevolent frenzy.
A crisp white sheet,
drying, by the soft amber of the afternoon sun, swaying
thoughtlessly,
in a gentle breeze.
An old reclusive farmhouse,
your safe, secret place.
But he finds you, even here.
He, a crusted shadow, needling, culling, plucking you from your
reverie.

A primal pant, paired with a dark, red Malbec. The crunching sound,
single pane windows make, as they fold upon themselves.
The holes left behind, in the pretty, pistachio walls.
You, *pauvre petite souris,*
scurrying about the darkened pantry.
Close your eyes. Tight tight tight.
The distant laugh of your children,
the hands of your mother, the face of your father, with vacant,
brittle sockets, of abandoned flesh.
A tempest is never sorry for its lightning. The eerie bright,
the slumbered aftermath,
a limbless caricature in its wake.
A forced sojourn.
A reluctant abdication.
Sorrowful storm chaser,
marooned in perpetual wait.

REAL MONSTERS
by Jennifer Weigel

Don't lurk under the bed,
they slip quietly through
the bedroom door
under guise of
bringing
a glass
of water.

They stand staring,
unbuckling their belt,
unzipping pants,
while you pray
for them to
just go
away.

They sit at the head of the
dinner table and act
as though nothing
ever happened,
tell you to eat
your peas
or else.

They threaten you—
"Don't dare speak
a word of this…"
while you wish
beyond hope
it won't go
unnoticed.

TEN FEET UNTIL OBLIVION
by C.V. Hunt

Ten bodies long,
three bodies wide,
trapped in a tin can with a monster.

The gargoyle perched in his green recliner,
smoke pouring from his nostrils.
Staring at the flickering screen without seeing.
Smoking,
staring,
empty,
full of rage and alcohol.

On the inside, she is fear.
Numb.
On the outside, nothingness.
Longing for oblivion.

The door glows red-hot.
Salvation.
The oblivion maker.
If she leaves, she is free.
If she leaves, she will die.
Freedom though death or death for staying.

A hole in the head, he'd said,
tapping between her eyes with a nicotine-stained finger,
three inches right of the bruise.
A promise.

She waits,
stomach churning,
face aching,
fighting tears that will trigger the next strike.

A woman who cries for her mother.

Happy people do
happy things on the television.
Happy people cheer and clap and
no one in the room notices.

The doors says, freedom,
but she knows better.
She closes her eyes,
wishes she had the courage to end herself.
Wishes her mother could comfort her.

Ten feet between her and freedom but
he promises death instead.
Death on either side of the door,
slowly inside,
quick outside, before she can make it to the road.

THICKER THAN WATER
by Marie Lestrange

This cannot be my only son.
Innocence gone by
When first we laced your little shoes,
and now these knots you tied.

Around my wrists, my legs, my life
blood dripping to the floor.
I thought you were my angel,
yet your actions speak to more

First it was the animals.
Accidents! You cried.
Though I proclaimed your innocence then,
It is clear now that you lied.

The neighbor's bird and then that boy,
we thought he was your friend.
But with another accident
he swiftly met his end.

They lead to you, these terrible acts
My precious, vicious boy.
And when you heard we'd turn you in,
our saving grace, destroyed.

A Mother's fear, brought to light
of innocence no more.
And now I sit, beside your father
sprawled across the floor.

I am the next, of that I'm sure.
All memories betrayed.
Where once I craved your warming hugs,
but now, I am afraid.

Put down the knife, there's still a chance.
We can start again, anew.
Yet as you slither close, determined,
I know the words aren't true.

TO BE ALONE
by Miriam H. Harrison

in the beginning was
the word—*alone*

they said it is not good
to be alone, and so we
came together only to
fall away in
splinters

now these pieces are what
we have become—beams and specks
in each other's eyes, slivers
buried under skin burning sickly
red—all else gone the way of
matching socks and other
domestic casualties

I make the bed and find
a long-unanswered
I Love You among the pillows—
I cannot remember if it was yours or mine

in the silence of
our bed is the end, the
beginning, the word

alone

it is not good
to be alone, except
for when it is

ANYTHING CAN BE A WEAPON, BUT SOME THINGS CAN'T BE ANYTHING ELSE
by Amelia Gorman

If we got married in a horror movie
would I still let you pick up that ice pick
on our honeymoon?

    "Why did we come to Pompeii if not to see bodies?"
sea bodies writhing in the ash you add another lump of cold
to my Campari and soda and it bubbles after
bodies that intertwine without moving, without warmth
or with nothing keeping them together but warmth
like Fulci's fog-eyed couple.

If this were a novel with yellow pages
and a red and white title, below it
    "Bodies without limbs and limbs without bodies!"
in your red and white voice I would never
ever have asked you to split the wood,
never found the hatchet in the shed and I
would have rather stayed cold I think

but our wallpaper is yellow, and our staircase is crumbling and
our rocks
are not shaped for landscaping
    —and "pardon me—the director of my life says
—that's an unacceptable way" to talk about your role in this movie—

you, the box grater full of holes, you in the kitchen
full of weapon. weapon. Weapon.
Canola oil and ranges. Relief when the last cup of coffee in the day
is poured out, the credits roll,
and the killer steps into the camera
smiling to advertise the sequel.

ALMOST
by Sarah Edmonds

The screaming winter wind was almost enough.

Enough to drown out my cries,
Enough to freeze the feel of your touch from my skin,
Enough to make me numb.

Almost.
But as the Spring brings the thaw, I see

Almost is not enough.

BOUND BY SILVER
by Sharmon Gazaway

You've had me in your eye
for a while. That silver
slice in your wolf-amber
eyes calls to me
like frozen deep dark chocolate—

grizzled, close-buzzed beard
runs unkempt past your Adam's apple.
You scratch it lazily with the edge
of your nail, your lips
part in a smile so white
the teeth, I know, will bite sharp.

You take my hand and lead
me through woods
like it's your second home.
The air quivers with the dart
of nervous hares and the black
smoke wings of crows. My hand so snug
in yours, I pay no heed.
    Strolling back
the moon rises over your shoulder
as you press a ring of silver into my palm.

We wed under an ash tree
your tux, black as a growl
my gown lamb-white
ash-gold leaves fall around us—
a hungry nip in the air
both of us so lean

all friction and static electricity
and like the pent-up energy
in espresso at midnight
I'll be consumed.

Your hand on mine
across our breakfast table
you say *I love you*—
the glint in your pupils
like parentheses say
(*this could end badly*). I squeeze
your hand reassuringly
so you can feel the silver
bullet in my palm.

COLD SNAP
by Carol Edwards

His anger stills the house
like a pond before dawn,
the coldest moment of the night.

The dog hides under my desk,
a cave
where he cannot find him.

The cats collect across my carpet,
under the bookshelf leaves,
breath suspended, waiting.

A fly buzzes an audacious sacrilege,
smacks against window glass
desperate to escape,

> ripples the water tension
> under which
> the rest of us suffocates.

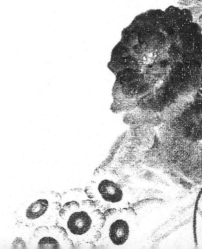

POEM: FAIRY TALES (VERSION: 1959)
by Debra Bennett

On the screen you have:
The white horse and the white sun,
The broken beat of retreating hooves
Into those red hills:
Rest dust and blood and, of course,

the bad guys vanquished
the good guys tall on their tall horses.

Afternoon you are twelve
and you have nothing,
Vancouver rain, two o-clock
you should be in school
but aren't, the seat slaps back behind you,
lights flicker on
to kids hidden
shivering inside
their jackets,
to those matrons
of the fifties
in their shabby
polyester coats.

Outside, on Georgia,
the watery shop windows
rush up behind you:

cars and lights flooding on
your small black-coated back
running and running

—go home, little girl
Go home to yet
another fairy-tale.
In this one, your father
is the big bad wolf
he's huffing and puffing
and beating down the doors.
In this one,
Your mother is sitting behind
a locked bath-room door
reading the writing
On the yellow walls.

You want to live somewhere else,
some other planet maybe
you want to swallow fire or your own blood
your cells shrinking slowly
to nothing

and there's always that soft black gun
on your cold cheek
the silent feet, the curtain edging back
to empty streets—
—and there should be some hero now
some hero thudding in on
his white horse to rescue you—
but the heroes are all
boarded up
behind windows, or gone away.

Gone away.

And your heart jumps back
like a bullet into
your own skinny chest,

and you are twelve again,
running through the streets
in the rain, to your parents
who are crying together
In another tired yellow room
and another
and another.

In your dream
your father is turning his hands
over and over
full of the red dust
and the blood, the wind rises
huffing and puffing
blowing out the lights along the block
where you run,
where you sit in a room
with your mother
reading the writing
on the yellow walls.

RED FLAGS
by Michelle Meyer

Lately, whenever we try
to discuss, there is no room
for anyone else. He is
in the way,
even of himself.
It has become easier for me
to sit back and watch,
as a spectator would, a sport.
He acts out all of the roles:
     Announcer.
     Player.
     Overly impressed audience member.
He monologues while I stare out the window
obsessing over butterflies, over how they repeatedly
land & fly away, land & fly away.
The simplicity of it makes me laugh, but
he doesn't hear me.
He drones and I say, *Um, hmmm,*
then reach for the remote
and absently press the OFF button
even though the TV isn't on.

WHO CARES FOR THESE WOMEN?
by Anna Bagoly

there is this idea
that people*
    *and of these people
    the majority are women
that people* who stay in abusive situations
    (for these can
    never be relationships)
do so because they are complacent
because their will isn't suited for independence
they need someone to direct,   govern,   give purpose

and not that these people* have already expended every piece of agency
in attempting to liberate themselves
that of course relationships never begin this way, with the
temperature slowly rising, when do you   notice a change?

that those whose every movement and thought
is pre-scripted
by themselves or their captor
    (as these are really more
    hostage situation
    aren't they?)
under threat of blackening-blossom skin
under threat of breakings
        of deportation
        of breathing their last by the other's arms

who cares for these women? about the abuse, who cares about what happens behind locked doors? who is going to help feed her kids, when she leaves, with nothing to her name? who cares about immigrant women whose words spill not in english? who speaks for the most vulnerable, when they are under ten feet of water every day? when opening her mouth means drowning?

WOMEN ON ICE
by Roni Stinger

She's dead again. Killed in a million brutal ways. Her name
doesn't matter. Interchangeable faces, all of them pretty.

Mouth shut. Eyes wide. Pale rigid skin flawless. Crystalline
shards under her nails. She didn't fight, too unladylike.

Don't fear. The hero will come to her rescue. Kill the bad
guy. Win the glory. She'll stay in the fridge, suspended.

For a fee, he'll show you his prize. Look at her frozen
expression. Her vapid stare. Knees bent at odd angles,

never managed in life. Tiny mouths formed by thousands
of wounds, scream out to all who might hear.

HOUSE
by Donna Lynch

For every ugly thing
I ever did
and every ugly thing
done unto me
I built a room
without a blueprint
without a permit
And I'm no Mrs. Winchester
but this house has gotten rather large
and is painted with regret
in every shade of red
and truly makes no sense
to anyone
but me
And yes
I know
it looks so haunted
from the outside
but the only ghost here
is the structure
itself.

AN ACT OF CONTRITION
by S. Creaney

My fingernails are sticky notes painted and chalked to remind me
to pick myself up after myself.
You don't like old molars in the sink,
lungs drying on the windowsill
while marbles line my gums and void my excuses.
We all live differently.
Not everyone is cobbled together from rock and scald.
My eyes don't even see in shapes or colors,
just feelings and suspicions.

As in: I suspect you'll break my ribs
when you reach clumsily for your glass and hit my heart instead.
My own fault,
of course,
for placing the shots in my chest and forgetting my heart on the
table
amongst the detritus of plastic and paper and the scum atop ponds.
And you're drunk so apologies are pointless
since you'd never know the difference either way.
Whiskey from the glass,
the bottle,
or from me still tastes like whiskey.
It still burns and cleans and saves the soul
like a baptism in sea salt winter water.

RESTING FACES
by Rebecca Thrush

There is a mask I wear sat neatly upon this face
Round and plump, I am pinked like a peach
In the flash of a candle I might still be here
Quiet eyes hidden underneath
But the face you see is not my own
It feels of rubber, as it mimics me—
Stapled dimples on stacks of flesh
You smile, wave, and it bounces
right back at you. Can you see
my edges peeling? Do you know
where this face ends and I begin?
Some days I know I'll never find myself
sitting here as a stranger in my own home

THE FIRST CUT IS THE DEEPEST
by Rie Sheridan Rose

The first cut is the deepest...
because it is a surprise.
You thought he was your soulmate—
you thought you'd be together forever,
joined at the hip
to battle life's dragons...
But one night you drop a glass,
and he makes you kneel on the shards
to clean it up...
crimson staining the broken dream.
He blames it on stress at work—
and you forgive him...
because you love him.
The next cut comes when you are late
returning from a well-deserved lunch
with the friend you've known
since high school.
He's not even supposed to be home
on a work day.
He slaps you across the face
because there was no waiting meal...
though you'd made him a lunch
to carry with him.
Dreading the answer,
you ask him why he's come home—
and earn another blow.
His manager's a cunt, he says...
and the security of pension and pay
evaporates like smoke.

His temper burns like fire within him
and you start at every shadow…
The happy home you dreamed of
stinks of beer and despair.
The bruises are no longer surprises…
His demon was well hidden when you met,
but now it is loose.
It rages against you—beating you down
with his familiar frame.
The battle must end…
either in flight or death.
How will you choose?

MIRROR, MIRROR
by Carol Gyzander

Mime, trapped in the mirror
Hands pressed against the glass
My face silently screaming
    Unheard in the conversation

You paid so much attention at first
A whirlwind of fun things to enjoy
Keen interest in what I was doing
    I felt so valued, truly seen

We grew closer and shared so much
I threw open the window to my soul
Until subtle changes crept in
    The focus started to shift

More and more talk about you
The burdens you carried
How much you went through
    No one understood you

I became flat, my surface reflective
You looked in my window frame
And saw only yourself
    My own image disappeared

If I didn't reflect enough attention
The rage, the rage
I'm in a bad way here, you'd say
    But what did that really mean?

My needs and interests devalued
Couldn't possibly be as important
I should just recognize
    That it was all about you

I tried to pantomime what I needed
Such an insult to you
The rage, the threats!
    You pointed out that mirrors can crack

My call to the police was a betrayal
You said you were misunderstood
How dare I worry about my own safety
    Couldn't I tell you had it all under control?

Control—yes, that's what it was
The balance had shifted from our mutual gaze
To where it was all about you
    All about you

But friends dusted off my surface
And made me remember
I had been multi-dimensional
    I could have my own image again

Together we broke the mirror's frame
I left while you were away
Because it's not all about you
    It's not all about you

It's not.

CURED
by Melody Alice

no longer suffering she said
as she updated my file
I could see in her confident smile
that she had never known
the dread of the front lock turning
heavy boots in the hallway
precisely timed hot meals
that the entire world could collapse with
only a disappointed sigh

what a relief I thought
to be cured
as my rabbit heart beat fast and steady
and I smiled back

AT THE THRESHOLD
by Jennifer Fischer

he comes to the threshold of the door, but doesn't enter
every night
okay, some nights he enters
long after I've gone 'to sleep'

but who sleeps anymore?
me?
sometimes
certainly not him, crawling into bed at 5 or 6 in the morning, as
I begin to contemplate starting my day

what is there to start?

or, he enters the room while I am still clearly awake
he wants to reach out, make some gesture, but does not
it's just as well
I would not receive, accept or reciprocate

often, I imagine he enters when I am truly asleep
puts his hands around my neck and contemplates pressure
or places a pillow onto my face
ready to put us both out of our misery
but he doesn't have the courage

to strangle, to suffocate, to blow his brains out

his brains out
the image that plagues my sleep

he wipes his oil-stained hands on the faded red rag he always
carries in his back pocket

but his hands never come clean
I dust the urn on the mantel
but it never shines
never reflects back what I want to see

I try crawling inside the urn
becoming one with my son again
as when I carried him in my womb
we don't fit

and I don't have the courage either
to follow him

this is my penance, I think
this is what I deserve
this empty house
this empty man locked inside with me
and the ashes of our dead son

WHEN I OPEN THE DOOR
by Melodie Bott

One
When I open the door,
a stranger greets me on the porch,
tousled hair, swollen watermelon face,
blood bubbles on her lip.
As she says hello, her voice startles my soul.
I know this wreck of a woman.
My friend sleeps on the couch. In the morning,
she returns to him.

Two
When I open the door,
My friend's ratted hair
whips across her gaunt face
Eggplant shadows root under her eyes.
She licks cracked, scabbed lips.
She won't come in. Instead,
her tears soak the porch. Cradling her wrist,
she goes to him.

Three
When I open the door, my gossamer friend
greets me on the porch. Her skull, earth-quaked,
holds little skin. A few strands of blood matted hair
drift over eye sockets bubbling with void.
Blood stains root her shirt over ribbons of ribs.
My silent voice anchors her soul from Heaven.
And she stays with him.

THERE'S NO PLACE LIKE HOME
by Renee Cronley

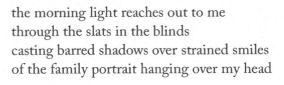

the morning light reaches out to me
through the slats in the blinds
casting barred shadows over strained smiles
of the family portrait hanging over my head

I disappear a little more everyday
in this household made of me
pieces of my body and intelligence
he bit out between kisses and compliments
so I never noticed when
the best parts of me went missing

now I am a relic of the goddess I was
desolate ruins in a state of decay
the dust tries to leak out my eyes
and I have to force them shut

the air is heavy with lemon-scented bleach
and all the emotions I refuse to feel
they seep out my pores and dew his skin
he wipes them away until he can't anymore

he stomps over the welcome mat
under the influence of himself
with sentimental quotes written on décor
he hammers into the wall with sharp nails
while chewing out the mess of me
before cleaning me up off the floor
as we bond over my tears and apologies

when night comes to black out the day
he steals me to our marriage bed
and I fall asleep in the soft restraints of his arms
until daybreak whispers my eyes open
and morning light tries to reach out to me again

WHEN HE COMES TO ME HALF-ANIMAL
by Laura Cranehill

in the dark of room
me a mouse drowning in a wine bottle
I never know what to do, because

the fear but mostly shame, always shame
with the tiny fears, tiny in the shame
I am a mouse, mouse
and sometimes the house is so big
and he comes to me and opens my skin
and shuffles in the shadow pockets of my body, finding
constellations
and it calms him
and it calms me
until the sea builds again

When did I return
to being a child?
Lost in all the loving hate and confusion, unable to argue
my own terms of living? Placating, placating
so I can breathe
so I can be given room to be
until

the dark sea-wine toss in the bed
we become connected again, briefly
his animal folded up neatly inside him until morning
when the beast limbs unfurl, rise
as hardened bone and sinew and tusk
and I am a mouse, curling up
to find a cavity
of breath

GHOST
by Rebecca Dietrich

Your ghost haunts me
Even though
I'm the one who left
The rattle of the chains
You placed on my heart
Echoes in the night
I still see your face
With that deceiving grin
In my nightmares
Your lingering spirit
Lives on in my mind
Rest In Peace
For I am not

BETTER HOMES AND GARDENS
by Ruth Towne

Inside the calmest eye of hurricane, we talk
of weather. Hello, the sun is out again. Wind
and pressure shift to drive inside spiders, ants,

and other insects. The weather orders their lives,
the weather scaffolds our platitudes. Frogs croak
from the lagoon, signal rain, monsoon. A spider

climbs the white sides of my tub. I do not drown
the spider, but I do not pick it up. No, I trap it
in a cup until the lack of air kills, not me. So ends

our friendship. How are you? Dew is on the grass,
rain will not come to pass. Rain three days, I want
us over quickly, abandoning any blame. Drawers,

doors all stick before rain. I introduce myself again.
Won't you ask me how I am? A spider's touch
remains long after the arachnid has gone. You feel

it too? At my ankles and wrists its touch persists.
The weather doesn't change. I have nothing left
to say. Still, I wonder this—if the winds reverse,

if I find you trapped like that spider inside my tub,
and you cannot flee my empty glass, will you learn
opposing pressures grow a cyclone? Within the eye

air sinks, blue sky silences violent wind. But winds
reverse, blame shifts, the eyewall's edge intensifies.
You are the spider, I the weather forcing you inside

to die. I clean my empty tub, set aside a special glass.
Another Noah to test the depths after a deluge,
I release spiders like white doves from my stoop.

BETTER
by Christina Sng

Two years later
And I am still broken,

My limbs—snapped branches
Askew in the dry mosses,
Bone-white and atrophied

Despite my repeated efforts
To revive, to resuscitate them,
One breath, one stretch at a time.

How easily things regress.
By the time you are fifty,
Your body conspires to kill you.

So I placate it
With loving words and gentle hugs.
This is my body. I am nothing without it.

I feed it dead things
And promises of restored glory.
It puts itself to work

And one day I see
Muscles on me,
My strength returning,

Adrenaline racing,
Jet fuel in a fighter plane
Raring to go to battle.

I am reenergized, recharged,
Fist waiting to mark his chest
With splatters of his own blood.

The blood eagle—
There is a sacredness to this ritual.
I tell him this

As his eyes widen and weep
Like the wounds he tore open
Whenever he needed his fix.

When the adrenaline wears off,
My pains return. But by this time,
He's already been cut open twice,

Breaking his spine, his lower body
Wrapped in a thick garbage bag
To contain the mess I will make.

First, I will show him I remember
All the cruel things he did to me
When we were together.

Then I will show him
I can do them better.

CARINA, CARINA
by Carina Bissett

Seeing stars, they call it,
as though cartoon characters
and spinning symbols
can capture a chokehold,
police lights shifting, spinning
from red to blue to red
haze, a starburst, vessels broken,
petechiae spotted on a field of white
surrender in the keelhauling,
barnacles replaced with the mundane,
chains wrought in butter knives,
jelly spoons scalloped.

Later, I learned my name exists
in a ridge of cartilage located
low in the trachea.
It lies past the throat,
between the division
where the airways bifurcate,
travelling in opposite directions,
a subterranean system leading to lungs
that once bellowed, screamed for help
until the loop closed, strangled.
The next breath nebulous,
subdued, drowned by sirens.

But there is another course, another Carina—
a constellation sailing southern skies,
centered by a solitary star,
a supergiant in her class,
a million times brighter than Earth's Sun,
    and I am reborn, radiant.

A MAP OF THE BACKYARD
by Jessica McHugh (Featured Poet)

Feminine as the grave,
You are blushing dirt combed over a bad dream.
Oh how you sparkle,
like a halo, red and spreading:
a stain with a name
Hanging like sweat around a boy's neck
after a night of catching fireflies
                        like you.

You were made for him, he said.
Like   a sculpture in the foyer
              a perfectly mixed martini
              a prescription, promptly filled

He took you like medicine:
the cure for a chronic illness flaring with promises
to loosen the mason jar lid
sealing his wounds while closing you in.
He kept his word the way he kept the house dark and quiet
So you didn't fear the showdown in his kiss
or find the poetry
        in your panic.

You were made for him, he insisted.
Like   a pearl plucked from the surf
              a secret kind of laughter
              a spiritual mantra

He rang the church bells in you
The way a lid seals a firefly in a jar:
It shines until it can't.
But panic is a secret kind of laughter too.
It's a play—right stage, wrong scene—
not performed but opened
like the First Wound, which, for some,
                    the weeping never stops.

Let panic twist the lid for you.
Draw the shades, clean the sheets.
Bundle up the fragments of a former life
And climb out of the dark.
Oh how you sparkle,
like his halo, red and spreading,
more name than stain.
He burned so many holes in you,
There are plenty of places to bury him.

ABOUT THE EDITORS

Lindy Ryan is a Bram Stoker Awards®-nominated and award-winning editor, author, director, and professor. In 2017, Ryan founded Black Spot Books, an award-winning independent small press, specializing in horror and dark fantasy, where she maintains her role as President after the company was acquired in 2019 as an imprint of Vesuvian Media Group. In 2020, Ryan was named a *Publishers Weekly* 2020 Star Watch Honoree. She is a regular contributor at *Rue Morgue*, *Booktrib*, and *LitReactor*, and has been featured in *NPR*, *BBC Culture*, *Irish Times*, *Daily Mail*, *Fangoria*, and more. In 2022, Ryan was named one of horror's most masterful anthology curators, and has been declared a "champion for women's voices in horror" by Shelf Awareness (2023). Read more at lindyryanwrites.com.

Lee Murray is a multi-award-winning writer and poet, and a five-time Bram Stoker Awards® winner, including for poetry for *Tortured Willows: Bent, Bowed, Unbroken*, a collaborative title with Christina Sng, Angela Yuriko Smith, and Geneve Flynn. A Grimshaw-Sargeson Fellow and Laura Solomon Cuba Press Prize-winner for her prose poetry manuscript *Fox Spirit on a Distant Cloud*, Lee is an NZSA Honorary Fellow and an Elgin, Rhysling, Dwarf Star, and Pushcart-nominated poet. Her poem "cheongsam" won her the Australian Shadows Award for 2021. Read more at leemurray.info.

ABOUT LYNNE HANSEN

Lynne Hansen is a horror artist who specializes in book covers. Her art has appeared on the cover of the legendary *Weird Tales Magazine*, and she was selected by Bram Stoker's great-grandnephew to create the cover for the 125th Anniversary Edition of *Dracula*. She has illustrated works by *New York Times* bestselling authors, including Jonathan Maberry, Brian Keene, and Christopher Golden, and created the cover art for *Under Her Skin*, the first book in Black Spot Books' women-in-horror poetry showcase series. Her art has been commissioned and collected throughout the United States and overseas. For more information, visit LynneHansenArt.com.

ABOUT SARA TANTLINGER

Sara Tantlinger is the author of the Bram Stoker Awards®-winning *The Devil's Dreamland: Poetry Inspired by H.H. Holmes*, and the Stoker Awards®-nominated works *To Be Devoured* and *Cradleland of Parasites*. She has also edited *Not All Monsters* and *Chromophobia*. She embraces all things macabre and can be found lurking in graveyards or on Twitter @SaraTantlinger, at saratantlinger.com and on Instagram @ inkychaotics.

ABOUT THE FEATURED POETS

Jessica McHugh is an award-nominated poet, novelist, and internationally produced playwright with twenty-nine books published in fourteen years, including her blackout poetry collection, *A Complex Accident of* Life, her sci-fi romp, *The Green Kangaroos*, and her horror series, *The Gardening Guidebooks Trilogy*. Explore the growing worlds of Jessica McHugh at McHughniverse.com.

Marge Simon is a writer/poet/illustrator living in Ocala, FL, USA. A multiple Bram Stoker Awards®-winner and Grand Master of SFPA, her works appear in *Asimov's*, *Daily Science Fiction*, *Silver Blade*, *Magazine of F&SF*, more as well as anthologies such as *Birthing Monsters* and *What Remains* (Firbolg Publishing). Art galleries: http://www.margesimon.com.

Stephanie M. Wytovich is a novelist, essayist, and a Bram Stoker Awards®-winning poet. Her nonfiction craft book, *Writing Poetry in the Dark*, is now available from Raw Dog Screaming Press, and you can find her at http://stephaniewytovich.blogspot.com/ and on Twitter and Instagram @SWytovich and @thehauntedbookshelf.

ABOUT THE POETS

Melody Alice is a voice actor and author. She can currently be heard breathing life into LGBTQIA+ romance, thriller, and suspense literature. She writes and records from her historic and definitely not haunted Victorian manor in Kansas, supported by her partner, small army of foster cats, and rescue bunny. melodyalicevo.com.

Raina Allen is a young emerging poet, born and raised in Pennsylvania. She is a strong advocate for women's rights and mental health, and often uses her poetry as a vehicle to discuss her own experience with these issues. Her work has also been featured in *God's Cruel Joke* magazine.

Colleen Anderson is a multiple award nominee. Her poems have been published in seven countries in such venues as *Shadow Atlas*, *Brave New Weird*, *Future Fire*, and *HWA Poetry* Showcase. Her collection, *I Dreamed a World*, is available from LVP Publications, with *The Lore of Inscrutable Dreams* due in 2023 from Yuriko Publishing.

Anna Bagoly is a Hungarian-American writer. They are fascinated with recreating memories that immerse in sensation and imagery, blending poetry and creative nonfiction to create new forms. They've been published in *dead peasant* and *Heavy Feather Review* and have recorded a piece with the Mississippi Coalition Against Sexual Assault.

Alison Bainbridge is a poet and author living in Newcastle. Her poetry has been published in *Glitchwords*, *Wormwood Press Magazine*, *The Minison Project*, *Brave Voices Magazine*, and *Off Menu Press*, while her short stories have appeared in *Daughters of Darkness* (2019) ed. Blair Daniels, *Mirror Dance Fantasy*, and *Revenant Journal*.

Debra Bennett was an Early Childhood Educator for many years. She has published poetry in various magazines and journals: *The New Quarterly*, *The Capilano Review*, *West Coast Review*, *The Last Girls' Club*, and short fiction in others. She lives on Salt Spring Island, BC with her husband.

Carina Bissett is a writer and poet working primarily in the fields of dark fiction and fabulism. Her work has been published in multiple journals and anthologies including *Upon a Twice Time, Bitter Distillations: An Anthology of Poisonous Tales*, and *Arterial Bloom*. Her poetry has been nominated for the Pushcart Prize and can be found in the *HWA Poetry Showcase, Fantasy Magazine*, and *NonBinary Review*. She is also the co-editor of the award-winning anthology *Shadow Atlas: Dark Landscapes of the Americas*. http://carinabissett.com.

Amanda M. Blake is a cat-loving daydreamer and mid-age goth who loves geekery of all sorts, from superheroes to horror movies, urban fantasy to unconventional romance. She's the author of such horror titles as *Nocturne* and *Deep Down* and the fairy tale mash-up series *Thorns*.

Melodie Bolt is a Flint, Michigan poet who has appeared in venues such as *Prairie Schooner, Verse Wisconsin*, and *Horror Curated*. She is a decade-long member of Flint Area Writers, a member of the Great Lakes Association of Horror Writers, and lifetime member of SFPA. Her debut novel, *Fix*, was published in December 2022. She earned an MFA in Writing from Pacific University in Portland, Oregon. She currently resides with her partner, daughter, three dogs, and a kitty named Nyx. You can find her on Facebook or her website www.melodiebolt.com.

Wendy BooydeGraaff's poems have been included in *The Shore, Slant, About Place Journal, Plainsongs*, and elsewhere. Her fiction will be included in the forthcoming anthology *The Haunted States of America* (Henry Holt, 2024), and she is the author of *Salad Pie* (Chicago Review Press/Ripple Grove Press), a children's picture book.

Tiffany Michelle Brown is a California-based writer who once had a conversation with a ghost over a pumpkin beer. She is the author of the collection *How Lovely to Be a Woman: Stories and Poems* and co-host of the Horror in the Margins podcast.

Victorya Chase is a writer, artist, and educator who lives within the United States. Her novella, *Marta Martinez Saves The World* was published by Apokrupha, and she has numerous stories in journals and anthologies. Her Non-fiction writing about the journey through and with PTSD can be found in *Ninth Letter*, *WaterStone Review*, and other literary journals.

Alexis Clare is a multi-time published author, with their poetry books *The Sun And The Moon* series and numerous poetry through literary journals. They started writing poetry as a young adult, and it has kept them alive until today. They hope their writing can save themself and save the world at the same time.

Jude Clee is an educator and writer based in Philadelphia. Under her pseudonym, I write for the autism advocacy blog *Neuroclastic*. Her short story "The Boy in the Mirror" recently won a prize from Writer's Digest. "Hysteria" is her first poem.

A resident of Canberra, **PS Cottier** has published eight books of poetry. She also writes book reviews and the occasional short story. A keen collector of garden gnomes, PS Cottier also searches for the perfect 1980s jumper, with as many clashing colours as possible.

Laura Cranehill is a Pushcart-nominated writer based in Portland, OR where she lives with her partner and three sons. Her work has appeared in *Strange Horizons*, *Abyss & Apex*, *The Future Fire*, and elsewhere. She's currently wondering what to do with the placenta in her freezer.

S. Creaney has published short fiction in *Sword and Sorcery Magazine* and *Ripe Fiction*, poetry in *Poetry Shed* and with Black Spot Books, and had writing performed in off-Broadway theaters The Tank and The Poor Mouth. She teaches writing at the City College of New York and storytelling with The Moth, where some of her spoken word pieces can be found.

Renee Cronley is a writer and nurse from Manitoba. She studied Psychology and English at Brandon University, and Nursing at Assiniboine Community College. Her work appears or is forthcoming in *Chestnut Review*, *PRISM International*, *Off Topic*, *Love Letters to Poe*, and several other anthologies and literary magazines. Twitter & Instagram @reneecronley.

An author, poet, and editor, **Lauren Elise Daniels** won the 1987 Newport Poetry Prize and earned her MFA from Emerson College. Her novel, *Serpent's Wake: A Tale for the Bitten*, explores post-traumatic growth. Lauren's grandmother, a fierce spirit, was arrested more than once in 1930's NYC fighting for worker's rights.

Elizabeth Devecchi holds a French degree from Wittenberg University, a Law Degree from the University di Torino, Italy, and an LL.M. in International Law from The University of Iowa College of Law. Author of themoonthesunandlittleman.com, she is honored to make her poetry debut for this worthy cause.

Rebecca Dietrich is a writer from New Jersey. She has been published in *Plumwood Mountain Journal*, *Making Waves: A West Michigan Review*, and *Central Dissent*. Rebecca holds a B.A. in Psychology from Stockton University and is a graduate student at Keene State College's M.A. in Genocide Prevention program.

Sarah Edmonds is a queer author and filmmaker from southeastern Pennsylvania who specializes in all combinations of fantasy, horror, and queer fiction. Her debut novella, *Late Nights at Full Moon Records*, released September 2023 by Thirty West Publishing House, embodies everything she loves about exploring queerness through the horror genre.

Carol Edwards is a northern California native transplanted to southern Arizona. Her poetry has appeared in several publications, including *Space & Time*, *POETiCA REViEW*, and *White Stag Publishing*. Her debut collection, *The World Eats Love* was published by Ravens Quoth Press in April 2023. Instagram @practicallypoetical, Twitter and Facebook @practicallypoet.

Tracy Fahey is an Irish writer of prose and poetry. She has been twice shortlisted for Best Collection at the British Fantasy Awards in 2017 and 2022. Fahey's short fiction is published in over thirty American, British, Australian, and Irish anthologies. Her Guest of Honour spots include the UK Ghost Story Festival 2022 and Copenhagen Fantasticon 2023. Fahey holds a PhD on the Gothic in visual arts, and her non-fiction writing on the Gothic and folklore has appeared in edited collections. She has been awarded residencies in Ireland and Greece and most recently Saari Fellow status for 2023 by the Kone Foundation, Finland.

Alyson Faye lives near Brontë territory in the UK. She is a tutor, editor, parent, and dog walker. Her poetry has been widely published, and her poetry collection will be coming out with Brigids Gate Press. She loves old movies and drinking mead.

Jennifer Fischer is a creator whose films have been featured by NBCLatino, ABC, Univision, Fusion, NBCBLK, etc. Her writing has been featured by *Ms. Magazine*, *Literary Mama*, and others. She has an essay in *What is a Criminal? Answers from Inside the U.S. Justice System* (Routledge Press, 2023).

Geneve Flynn is a two-time Bram Stoker Awards® and Shirley Jackson Award-winning editor, author, and poet. Her works have been nominated and shortlisted for the British Fantasy, Ditmar, Aurealis, Australian Shadows, Elgin, and Rhysling Awards, and the Pushcart Prize. She is a recipient of the 2022 Queensland Writers Fellowship. Read more at www.geneveflynn.com.au.

M. Brett Gaffney is a queer poet and artist living in Salt Lake City, Utah with her family and their spoiled puggle, Ava. She holds an MFA in Poetry from Southern Illinois University, Carbondale, and her work has appeared in *Apex Magazine*, *Moon City Review*, *Zone 3*, *South Dakota Review*, *Devilfish Review*, and *Rust+Moth*, among other publications. Her chapbook *Feeding the Dead* (Porkbelly Press) was nominated for a 2019 Elgin Award from the Science Fiction and Fantasy Poetry Association.

Sharmon Gazaway is a 2022 Dwarf Stars Award finalist. Her work appears in *The Forge Literary Magazine*, *Daily Science Fiction*, *MetaStellar*, *The Fairy Tale Magazine*, *ParABnormal*, and elsewhere. Her work is featured in the award-winning *Love Letters to Poe Volumes 1* (and 2), and *New Myths' The Cosmic Muse*. You can find her work in anthologies published by Air and Nothingness Press, Brigids Gate Press, Ghost Orchid Press, and others. Sharmon writes from the Deep South of the US where she lives beside a historic cemetery haunted by the wild cries of pileated woodpeckers. Instagram @sharmongazaway.

Emma J. Gibbon is a horror writer and poet. Her poetry has been published in magazines and anthologies, including *Strange Horizons* and *Under Her Skin*. Emma lives with her husband and four exceptional animals—Odin, Mothra, Hamlet, and Grim—in a spooky house in the woods. Find her online at emmajgibbon.com.

Jessica Gleason is a writer, reader, professor, and an all-around weirdo. She loves horror and fantasy in their various shapes and forms, sometimes sleeps in a Star Trek uniform, and sings a mean hair metal karaoke. For daily updates, please follow her on Instagram (@j.g.writes).

Patricia Gomes, the first female Poet Laureate of New Bedford, Massachusetts (2014, 2021), has an abnormal interest in werewolves and is loath to write her bio. Playwright and the author of four poetry chapbooks, her work appears in numerous anthologies, both digitally and in print.

Amelia Gorman lives in Eureka, California where she spends her free time exploring tidepools and redwoods with her dogs and foster dogs. Her fiction has appeared in *Nightscript 6*, *Cellar Door* (Dark Peninsula Press), and *She Walks in Shadows* (Innsmouth Free Press). You can read her recent poetry in *New Feathers*, *Vastarien*, and *Penumbric*. Her first chapbook, the Elgin-winning Field Guide to *Invasive Species of Minnesota*, is available from Interstellar Flight Press.

Kerri Leigh Grady is a professional nerd permanently stressed out in the PNW. Find her at klgrady.com unless the site is down, in which case you should write her angry emails about it. Or don't. KL is probably too busy stressing out to read email. But, ya know, give it a shot?

H. Grim is a queer, chronically ill writer living in Canada with a house full of wild creatures, two of which were cut from her insides. When not writing, she's probably adventuring in a moody forest somewhere. You can find her enthusiastically yelling about books on social media as @The_GrimDragon.

Bram Stoker Awards®-nominee **Carol Gyzander** writes and edits horror and science fiction. She focuses on strong women with twisted tales that touch your heart. Her cryptid novella *Forget Me Not* occurs near Niagara Falls in 1969/1939; her latest horror anthology, *A Woman Unbecoming*, benefits reproductive healthcare services. CarolGyzander.com.

Kay Hanifen was born on Friday the 13th and lived for three months in a haunted castle. Her work has appeared in over forty anthologies and magazines. When she's not consuming pop culture with the voraciousness of a vampire at a 24-hour blood bank, you can find her at kayhanifenauthor.wordpress.com.

Amanda Hard holds an MFA in creative writing from Murray State University. Her work has appeared in numerous magazines and anthologies including *Lost Signals* and *Midnight in the Pentagram*. She is a staff writer for the web series, Still Water Bay, and lives in the cornfields of southern Indiana.

Linda Kay Hardie writes horror, crime, and fantasy stories, poetry, and fiction for children. Her writing has won awards dating back to a fifth-grade essay on fire safety. Linda has a master's degree in English from University of Nevada, Reno, where she teaches required courses to unwilling students.

Miriam H. Harrison writes among the boreal forests and abandoned mines of Northern Ontario, Canada. Her writings vary between the eerie, the dreary, and the cheery, and she is a regular contributor to Pen of the Damned. Find her on Facebook for ongoing updates about her work.

Roberta Whitman Hoff's work has appeared in *Caduceus, Fresh Ink,* and *Freshwater*. Roberta has a Bachelor of Arts and has taken poetry workshops with distinguished poets such as Dick Allen, Maria Luisa Arroyo, and Margaret Gibson. During the pandemic, she returned to her love of Gothic and revisited books like Bram Stoker's *Dracula* and Mary Shelley's *Frankenstein* with a community of kindred gothic and horror readers online at The Rosenbach.

D. C. Houston is a writer and poet from Kincardine, Ontario, Canada. Her passion for finding words to describe the human condition has led her to be included in multiple successful anthologies. Her latest poem, "Stjärna/Pretty Star Baby", is being sent in the Polaris Time Capsule to the Lunar South Pole aboard SpaceX/Astrobotic Griffin/NASA Viper Rover in 2024. You can follow her journey on Instagram.

Juleigh Howard-Hobson's work can be found in *The Deadlands, Polu Texni, 34 Orchard, Midnight Echo, The Lost Librarian's Grave* (Redwood Press), *Under Her Skin* (Black Spot Books) *Vastarien: Women's Horror* (Grimscribe), and other venues. Her latest collection is *Curses, Black Spells and Hexes* (Alien Buddha Press). She tweets @poetforest.

C.V. Hunt is the author of twenty books, including *Ritualistic Human Sacrifice* and *Halloween Fiend*. They are also the owner and head editor of Grindhouse Press. You can sign up to their newsletter at www.cv-hunt.com.

Sarah Jane Huntington is the author of several short story collections, novellas, and novels. Her work has appeared in multiple anthologies. She is a nurse and lover of animals.

Frances Lu-Pai Ippolito is a Chinese-American writer in Portland, Oregon. Her writing has appeared or is forthcoming in several venues including *Nightmare Magazine*, Flame Tree Press anthologies, and

Unquiet Spirits. Frances co-chairs the Young Willamette Writers program that provides free writing classes for high school and middle school students.

Vanessa Jae writes horrifically beautiful anarchies, reads stories for *Apex Magazine*, and is poetry editor at *Strange Horizons*. She also collects black hoodies and bruises in mosh pits on Tuesday nights. To read tweets by interesting people follow her at @thevanessajae.

Ai Jiang is a Chinese-Canadian writer, a Nebula Award finalist, and an immigrant from Fujian. She is a member of HWA, SFWA, and Codex. Her work can be found in *F&SF, The Dark, Uncanny*, among others. She is the recipient of Odyssey Workshop's 2022 Fresh Voices Scholarship and the author of *Linghun* and *I AM AI*. Find her on Twitter (@AiJiang_) and online (http://aijiang.ca).

Jo Kaplan is the author of *It Will Just Be Us* and *When the Night Bells Ring*. Her fiction has appeared in *Fireside, Black Static, Nightmare, Vastarien, Nightscript*, and elsewhere. She is the co-chair of the HWA LA chapter and teaches English and creative writing at Glendale Community College.

Vivian Kasley hails from the land of the strange and unusual, Florida. She's a writer of short stories and poetry. Some of her street cred includes Brigids Gate Press, Grimscribe Press, Ghost Orchid Press, The Denver Horror Collective, Death's Head Press, and poetry in Black Spot Books inaugural women in horror poetry showcase *Under Her Skin*. She has more in the works, including her first collection.

Naching T. Kassa is a wife, mother, and horror writer. She serves as an assistant at Crystal Lake Publishing and is a proud member of both the Horror Writers Association and Mystery Writers of America. You can find her work on Amazon at https://www.amazon.com/Naching-T-Kassa/e/B005ZGHTI0.

Sophie Kearing is a writer of dark poetry and fiction. Her work has been featured by *Lumiere Review, Horror Tree, Ellipsis Zine*, Roi Fainéant Press, *New Pop Lit, Isele Magazine, Pigeon Review,* Jolly Horror

Press, *Sazeracs Smoky Ink, Popshot Quarterly*, and other publications. She'd love to connect with you: https://twitter.com/SophieKearing.

Lindsay King-Miller is the author of *Ask a Queer Chick: A Guide to Sex, Love, and Life for Girls who Dig Girls* (Plume, 2016). Her fiction has appeared in *Fireside, Baffling Magazine*, and other publications. She lives in Denver, CO with her partner and their two children. Her debut horror novel, *The Z Word*, is forthcoming from Quirk Books in Spring 2024.

EV Knight is the author of the Bram Stoker Award®-winning debut novel *The Fourth Whore*. She released her sophomore novel *Children of Demeter* in August 2021 and is the author of three novellas, including her recently released autofiction, *Three Days in the Pink Tower*. She has also written several poems and short stories published in various anthologies. EV lives in one of America's most haunted cities: Savannah, GA. When not out and about searching for the ghosts of the past, she can be found at home with her husband, her beloved Chinese Crested, and their three naughty sphynx cats.

Nicole Kurtz is the recipient of the Ladies of Horror Grant, the HWA Diversity Grant, and a two-time Palmetto Scribe Award Winner. She's the editor of the groundbreaking anthology, *SLAY: Stories of the Vampire Noire*. She's written for *White Wolf, The Realm*, and *Baen*. She enjoys reading scary stories and mysteries.

Christina Ladd is a writer, reviewer, and editor living in Minneapolis. She will eventually die crushed under a pile of books, but until then you can find her work at christinaladd.com.

Pushcart Prize nominee, **Blaise Langlois**, lives in small-town Ontario. You will usually find her feverishly scratching out ideas after midnight. Her poems have been published by *Space and Time Magazine*, Black Spot Books, *Lothlorien Poetry Journal*, the Science Fiction and Fantasy Poetry Association and more. For links to her work, check out: www.ravenfictionca.wordpress.com.

Emma Lee's publications include *The Significance of a Dress* (Arachne, 2020) and "Ghosts in the Desert" (IDP, 2015). She co-edited *Over Land, Over Sea* (Five Leaves, 2015), was Reviews Editor for *The Blue Nib*, reviews for magazines and blogs at https://emmalee1.wordpress.com.

Dr. Marie Lestrange is an artist, musician, and author of historical Horror from East Tennessee. Her humorous debut, *T is for Torture*, is a parody ABC "children's" book written for adults. She also co-hosts the "Moths to the Flame" podcast, drawing inspiration from all things macabre. @lestrangebooks (Instagram, Twitter, TikTok).

V.H. Litzinger is an enrolled member of the Eastern Band of Cherokee Indians. Although still young, she has experienced many hardships which have come to shape who she is. It is through her work that she hopes to share and tell others that their experiences are not alone.

Poet-Author-Illustrator **Lori R. Lopez** received honors for books including *The Dark Mister Snark, An Ill Wind Blows, The Fairy Fly*, and *Darkverse: The Shadow Hours* (Elgin Award Nominee; Kindle Book Awards Finalist). Seven poems have been nominated for Rhysling Awards. Lori's work appears in numerous publications, among them HWA Poetry Showcases. www.fairyflyentertainment.com.

Donna Lynch is a three-time Bram Stoker Awards®-nominated dark fiction writer, designer, spoken word artist, and the singer and co-founder—along with her husband, artist and musician Steven Archer—of the dark electro-rock band Ego Likeness (Metropolis Records). Her written works include *Isabel Burning, Red Horses, Driving Through the Desert*, and the poetry collections *In My Mouth, Ladies & Other Vicious Creatures, Daughters of Lilith, Witches, Choking Back the Devil*, and *Girls from the County*. Her poems and short stories have appeared in several anthologies. She and her husband live in Maryland.

Caitlin Marceau is a queer author based in Montreal. She's an Active Member of the Horror Writers Association and has spoken about literature at several Canadian conventions. Her work includes

Palimpsest, Magnum Opus, Femina, and her debut novella, *This Is Where We Talk Things Out.* For more, visit CaitlinMarceau.ca.

Lana C. Marilyn is an interdisciplinary literary artist and writer of Afro-Caribbean descent from Brooklyn, NY. Her poetry is inspired by her love of speculative, surrealist film and a deep appreciation for internet culture. Find her on Twitter (@Cinniie).

Jeannie Marschall is a teacher from the green centre of Germany who also writes stories, time permitting. She enjoys long walks, foraging, and inventing tall tales with her partner. Jeannie mostly writes colourful, queer SFFH stories as well as the occasional poem. Twitter: @ JunkerMarschall or Mastodon: @JeannieMarschall@fandom.garden.

V.C. McCabe is the author of the forthcoming *Ophelia* (Femme Salve Books, 2023) and *Give the Bard a Tetanus Shot* (Vegetarian Alcoholic Press, 2019). Her work appears in journals such as *EPOCH, Poet Lore,* and *Coffin Bell.* An Appalachian poet, she has lived in Ireland and West Virginia. Site: vcmccabe.com. Twitter: @vcmpoetry.

Tiffany Meuret is the author of multiple works, including the novels *A Flood of Posies* and *Little Bird.* She lives in sunny Arizona with her husband, kids, and a menagerie of animals.

Michelle Meyer is the author of *10 Pieces of Truth,* a chapbook, and *The Book of She,* a full collection of character vignettes devoted to and illustrated by women. Her latest collection *The Trouble with Being a Childless Only Child* is forthcoming from Cornerstone Press.

Dawn McCaig is an Assistant Crown Attorney who prosecutes all manner of serious crime. She escapes the stress of her professional life by writing fiction. Her work has appeared in numerous publications. She lives in Nipissing District, Ontario, Canada.

Tiffany Morris is a Mi'kmaq writer of speculative fiction and poetry from Kjipuktuk (Halifax), Nova Scotia. She is the author of the horror poetry collection *Elegies of Rotting Stars* (Nictitating Books, 2022).

Her work has appeared in *Nightmare Magazine, Apex Magazine,* and *Uncanny Magazine,* among others. Find her at tiffmorris.com.

Emma E. Murray writes dark speculative fiction. Her stories have appeared in anthologies like *What One Wouldn't Do* and *Obsolescence,* and magazines such as *Pyre* and *If There's Anyone Left.* When she's not writing, she loves playing with her daughter and being a bard in D&D. To read more, visit EmmaEMurray.com or follow her on Twitter @ EMurrayAuthor.

Mim Murrells is from Essex. They are currently earning a BAH in English Literature with Creative Writing from the University of East Anglia in Norwich, where they live part-time. Their poetry can be read in *Wrongdoing Magazine, Corporeal Magazine,* and more. They are a proud parent to four terrible cats.

Victoria Nations writes Gothic horror and weird fiction, often with monsters. Her recent poetry appears in *Mother: Tales of Love and Terror, Magpie Messenger* literary journal, and *HWA Poetry Showcase, Volume IX.* She lives in Florida, USA, with her wife and son. Visit her at VictoriaNations.com and @Leaves_Cobwebs.

Cindy O'Quinn is a four-time Bram Stoker Awards®-Nominated writer. She is an Appalachian writer from West Virginia. Cindy now lives in Maine, on the old Tessier Homestead. It's the ideal backdrop for writing dark stories and poetry. Follow Cindy for updates: Facebook @CindyOQuinnWriter, Twitter @COQuinnWrites, and Instagram cindy.oquinn.

Abi Marie Palmer is a writer and English teacher from the UK. You can find more of her work at abimariepalmer.com

Stephanie Parent is an author of dark fiction and poetry. Her debut poetry collection *Every Poem a Potion, Every Song a Spell* was published by Querencia Press.

H.V. Patterson lives in Oklahoma and writes speculative poetry and fiction. Her poem, "Mother; Microbes" was selected for *Brave New Weird: The Best New Weird Horror* from Tenebrous Press. She promotes women in horror through @Dreadfulesque on Twitter and Instagram. She's on Twitter @ScaryShelley.

Jessica Peter writes dark, haunted, and sometimes absurd short stories, novels, and poems. She lives in Hamilton, Ontario, Canada. You can find her writing in *LampLight Magazine*, The NoSleep Podcast, and *Haven Speculative*, among other places. You can find more about her and her work at www.jessicapeter.net.

Marisca Pichette lingers in shadows. More of her work appears in *Strange Horizons, Vastarien, Apparition Lit, Flash Fiction Online*, and *PseudoPod*, among others. Her poetry collection, *Rivers in Your Skin, Sirens in Your Hair*, released from Android Press in April 2023.

Canadian author **Mary Rajotte** has a penchant for penning nightmarish tales of gothic and folk horror. Her fiction and poetry has been published in a number of anthologies and she is the creator of *Frightmarish: A Gothic LitZine*, featuring original prose, poetry, and other dark delights. Visit her online at http://www.maryrajotte.com.

Saba Syed Razvi, PhD is the author of "In the Crocodile Gardens" (Elgin Award-nominee), "heliophobia", "Limerence & Lux", "Of the Divining and the Dead", and "Beside the Muezzin's Call & Beyond the Harem's Veil", as well as other poetry, fiction, & essays. She's an Associate Professor of English & Creative Writing at the University of Houston in Victoria, TX. Her website is www.sabarazvi.com.

Rie Sheridan Rose's poetry appears in numerous publications, including *Speculative Poets of Texas, Vol. 1*; *Texas Poetry Calendar*, and *Under Her Skin*. A member of SFWA, HWA, and SFPA, she has authored six poetry chapbooks, twelve novels, and lyrics for dozens of songs. She tweets as @RieSheridanRose.

Belicia Rhea was born under a waning crescent moon in the Sonoran Desert. She writes horror, weird fiction, and poetry. You can find her at beliciarhea.com and read more of her poems published in *Nightmare Magazine*, *Wrongdoing Magazine*, and elsewhere.

Jessica Sabo is an LGBTQ+ poet whose poems have appeared in *45th Parallel Lit Mag* and Viewless Wings Press, among others. She has also authored a chapbook, *A Body of Impulse*, (dancing girl press & studio, 2021). She currently lives in Nevada with her wife and senior rescue dogs.

Lynne Sargent is a flying philosopher-poet-queen. Find their work in venues like *Augur* and *Strange Horizons*, or purchase their poetry collection, *A Refuge of Tales*, wherever books are found. For more, visit them on Twitter @SamLynneS or scribbledshadows.wordpress.com.

Author of the Imadjinn Award Finalist *Liar: Memoir of a Haunting* (Omnium Gatherum, 2021), the novella *As Fast as She Can* (Sirens Call Publications, 2022), a story collection, and other works, **E.F. Schraeder**'s work has appeared in many journals and anthologies. Schraeder believes in ghosts, magic, and dogs.

Ava Serra's works have been published in *Salt Hill Journal*, *NAILED*, *Open Minds Quarterly*, *Lavender Review*, among others. By drawing from their own experiences with marginalization, they strive to forge mainstream literary spaces for underrepresented individuals. They are a poetry student in the University of Maryland's MFA program.

Elizabeth Anne Schwartz, born on Friday the 13th, writes sapphic stories and dark, enchanting tales. She earned her BA in Creative Writing at Purchase College. Follow her on Twitter @elizanneschwa.

Syd Shaw writes about love, witchcraft, and body horror. She is Assistant Poetry Editor and Workshop Coordinator at *Passengers Journal* and has a degree in creative writing from Northwestern University. She has previously been published in *The Winnow*, *Cathexis Northwest*, *Ember Chasm*, *Waxing & Waning*, *Eclectica Magazine*, *Panoply Zine*, and *The London Reader*, among others. Syd's work can be found on Twitter @sidlantro or at https://sydshaw.carrd.co.

A native Floridian, **Crystal Sidell** grew up playing with toads in the rain and indulging in speculative fiction. Her work has appeared in *34 Orchard*, *Apparition Lit*, *diet milk*, *F&SF*, *Orion's Belt*, *The Sprawl Mag*, *Strange Horizons*, and others. You can find her online at https://crystalsidell.wixsite.com/mysite.

smeep lives in Northern Saskatchewan, Canada. She developed a writing habit decades ago but put it aside for more serious pursuits. Now she is learning how to write poetry. Her poems have been published in *Spring*, *PRISM International*, and *Etched Onyx Magazine*.

Christina Sng is the three-time Bram Stoker Awards®-winning author of *A Collection of Nightmares*, *A Collection of Dreamscapes*, and *Tortured Willows: Bent. Bowed. Unbroken.* Her poetry, fiction, essays, and art appear in numerous venues worldwide, including *Interstellar Flight Magazine*, *New Myths*, *Penumbric*, *Southwest Review*, and *The Washington Post*.

Shannon E. Stephan, a mother, teacher, and writer residing in Florida, penned her first poem at ten years of age to cope with the death of a loved one. Today, she writes about living with depression, anxiety, and post-traumatic stress disorder, all of which stem from decades of religious trauma.

Roni Stinger lives in the Pacific Northwest, USA with her husband and two cats. When not writing strange and dark things, she is often wandering the forests, beaches, and streets in search of shiny objects and creative sparks. Her work has appeared in various magazines and anthologies. You can find her at www.ronistinger.com and on Twitter @roni_stinger.

Angela Sylvaine is a self-proclaimed cheerful goth who writes horror fiction and poetry. Her debut horror-comedy novel, *Frost Bite*, and debut novella, *Chopping Spree*, are available now. Angela's short fiction has appeared in various publications and podcasts, including *Apex Magazine*, *Dark Recesses*, and The NoSleep Podcast. Her poetry has appeared in publications including *Under Her Skin* and *Monstroddities*. You can find her online angelasylvaine.com.

Rebecca Thrush grew up in central Massachusetts and currently works in property management. When not working she enjoys writing poetry, painting, and creating digital collages. Published pieces of hers can be found on Instagram @rebeleigh92.

Ruth Towne is a graduate of the Stonecoast MFA program. Her poetry has recently appeared in *Grim & Gilded, Plainsongs Poetry Magazine, New Feathers Anthology, The Orchards Poetry Review, The Decadent Review, Inlandia Literary Journal*, and *Beyond Words Literary Magazine*. She hopes someday to become a respected gardener.

Emily Ruth Verona is a Pinch Literary Award winner and a Bram Stoker Awards® nominee with work featured in *Under Her Skin, Lamplight Magazine, Mystery Tribune, The Ghastling, Coffin Bell, The Jewish Book of Horror*, and *Nightmare Magazine*. Her debut thriller, *Midnight On Beacon Street*, is expected from Harper Perennial in 2024. She lives in New Jersey with a small dog. For more visit www.emilyruthverona.com.

Emily Vieweg is a poet and writer originally from St Louis, Missouri. Her poetry collection *but the flames* is available through Finishing Line Press. Her work has been published in *North Dakota Quarterly, Soundings Review, Art Young's Good Morning*, and more. She lives in Fargo, ND with her two children.

Antonia Rachel Ward is an author of horror and Gothic fiction based in Cambridgeshire, UK. Her gothic horror novella, *Marionette*, was published by Brigids Gate Press in August 2022 and her short stories have been published in multiple anthologies. She is also the founder and editor-in-chief of Ghost Orchid Press.

A one-time teen mother and high school dropout, **Larina Warnock** holds a doctorate degree from Creighton University and serves as an educator on the Oregon coast. She lives with her husband, three dogs, and a turtle older than she is. She is a survivor of domestic violence.

Jennifer Weigel is a multi-disciplinary mixed media conceptual artist. Weigel utilizes a wide range of media to convey her ideas, including assemblage, drawing, fibers, installation, jewelry, painting, performance, photography, sculpture, video, and writing. Much of her work touches on themes of beauty, identity (especially gender identity), memory & forgetting, and institutional critique.

Jacqueline West's poetry has appeared in *Liminality, Star*Line, Dreams & Nightmares, Enchanted Living*, and *Strange Horizons*. She is also the author of the NYT-bestselling series *The Books of Elsewhere* and several other award-winning books for young readers. Jacqueline lives with her family in Minnesota. Find her online at jacquelinewest.com.

Cassondra Windwalker is the poet of full-length collections *The Almost-Children* and *tide tables and tea with god*, as well as the Helen Kay Chapbook Award-winning book *The Bench*. She writes full-time from the southern coast of Alaska and enjoys interacting with generally decent human and humanoids on Twitter and Tribel @WindwalkerWrite.

L. Marie Wood is an award-winning dark fiction author, screenwriter, and poet with novels in the psychological horror, mystery, and dark romance genres. She is also the founder of the Speculative Fiction Academy, an English and Creative Writing professor, and a horror scholar. Learn more at www.lmariewood.com.

Mercedes M. Yardley is a dark fantasist who wears poisonous flowers in her hair. She is the author of *Darling, Beautiful Sorrows, Apocalyptic Montessa and Nuclear Lulu, Pretty Little Dead Girls*, and won the Bram Stoker Award® for "Little Dead Red." You can find her at mercedesmyardley.com.

Harley Woods is a graduating student at Warren Wilson College. They seek to dive headfirst into the literary community upon graduation and reach as many eyes with their vivid and immersive writing as possible.

Louise Worthington is the author of seven novels and several collections of dark poetry and flash fiction. She is a member of the HWA and a regular contributor to Pen of the Damned. Louise lives in rural Shropshire in the UK with her family and animals. Linktr.ee/louiseworthington.

Sarah Yasin facilitates writing retreats and moonlights at a convenience store in the state of Maine. An advocate for quelling light pollution, she urges everyone to keep our night skies dark. Her writing has appeared in various publications including *Mad Scientist Journal* and the *Horror Writers Association Poetry Showcase*.

VIOLENCE AGAINST WOMEN:
LEARNING MORE AND GETTING HELP?
A STARTING POINT

If the poems in *Under Her Eye* have inspired you to take action to stop violence against women in your community or help someone you know who is a victim, here are a few starting points:

To learn more about violence against women and how to help victims worldwide, visit www.thepixelproject.net

> **If you are in Asia**, you can find a list of crisis helplines for women at https://asiapacific.unwomen.org/en/focus-areas/end-violence-against-women/shadow-pandemic-evaw-and-covid-response/list-of-helplines

> **If you are in Australia or New Zealand**, you can find a list of crisis helplines for women at https://matebystander.edu.au/support-service-information-australia-and-new-zealand/

> **If you are in Europe**, you can find a list of crisis helplines for women at https://www.coe.int/en/web/istanbul-convention/help-lines

> **If you are in North America**, you can find a list of crisis helplines for women at:
> **Canada:** https://dawncanada.net/issues/issues/we-can-tell-and-we-will-tell-2/crisis-hotlines/
> **USA:** http://domesticshelters.org

If none of the list above covers your country or area, follow The Pixel Project on Twitter at @PixelProject (https://twitter.com/PixelProject). We tweet out helplines for victims of VAW in 205 countries daily at eight PM Eastern Time and for victims in North America daily at ten AM Eastern Time.

For domestic violence and sexual assault helplines and resources in every UN-recognized country and territory in the world, visit https://nomoredirectory.org/. This resource hub was created by the NO MORE Foundation in partnership with the United Nations and the World Bank.